# TEACUP MALTESE
# AND TEACUP MALTESE DOGS

From Teacup Maltese Puppies to Teacup Maltese Dogs
Includes: Maltese Puppies, Teacup Maltese Dogs, Miniature Maltese,
Temperament, Care, And More!

By Susanne Saben
© DYM Worldwide Publishers

DYM Worldwide Publishers

ISBN: 978-1-911355-02-1

**Published by DYM Worldwide Publishers 2016.**

**Copyright and Trademarks.** This publication is Copyright 2016 by DYM Worldwide Publishers. All products, publications, software, and services mentioned and recommended in this publication are protected by trademarks. In such instance, all trademarks & copyright belonging to the respective owners. All rights reserved. No part of this book may be reproduced or transferred in any form or by any means, graphic, electronic, or mechanical, including but not limited to photocopying, recording, taping, scanning, or by any information storage retrieval system, without the written permission of the author. Pictures used in this book are royalty free pictures purchased from stock photo websites with full rights for use within this work.

**Disclaimer and Legal Notice.** This product is not legal or medical advice and should not be interpreted in that manner. You need to do your own due diligence to determine if the content of this product is right for you. The author, publisher, distributors, and or/affiliates of this product are not liable for any damages or losses associated with the content in this product. While every attempt has been made to verify the information shared in this publication, neither the author, publisher, distributors, and/or affiliates assume any responsibility for errors, omissions, or contrary interpretation of the subject matter herein. Any perceived slights to any specific person(s) or organization(s) are purely unintentional. We have no control over the nature, content, and availability of the websites listed in this book. The inclusion of any website links does not necessarily imply a recommendation or endorse the views expressed within them. DYM Worldwide Publishers takes no responsibility for, and will not be liable for, the websites being temporarily or being removed from the Internet. The accuracy and completeness of the information provided herein and opinions stated herein are not guaranteed or warranted to produce any particular results, and the advice or strategies, contained herein may not be suitable for every individual. The author, publisher, distributors, and/or affiliates shall not be liable for any loss incurred as a consequence of the use and application, directly or indirectly of any information presented in this work. This publication is designed to provide information in regards to the subject matter covered. The information included in this book has been compiled to give an overview of the topics covered. The information contained in this book has been compiled to provide an overview of the subject. It is not intended as medical advice and should not be construed as such. For a firm diagnosis of any medical conditions you should consult a doctor or veterinarian (as related to animal health). The writer, publisher, distributors, and/or affiliates of this work are not responsible for any damages or negative consequences following any of the treatments or methods highlighted in this book. Website links are for informational purposes only and should not be seen as a personal endorsement; the same applies to any products or services mentioned in this work. The reader should also be aware that although the web links included were correct at the time of writing they may become out of date in the future. Any pricing or currency exchange rate information was accurate at the time of writing but may become out of date in the future. The Author,

Publisher, distributors, and/or affiliates assume no responsibility for pricing and currency exchange rates mentioned within this work.

# Table of Contents

* * *

## Chapter 1 - Introducing The Teacup Maltese!

* * *

There's absolutely nothing about a Teacup Maltese that doesn't steal my heart! From their long, silky coats, expressive little eyes, and black button noses, this breed of dog is the perfect little bundle of energy and love.

I'm the proud owner of three little Miniature Maltese dogs, and they're my babies through and through. I wouldn't trade them for the world.

I was born and raised in Southern Georgia, and cute, tiny dogs are as much a part of Southern culture as sweet tea and biscuits. I'd always owned toy breeds, but it wasn't until four years ago, when I purchased my own small, cozy little home on the outskirts of Macon, that I decided that the time was right to expand my horizons and get a Miniature Maltese. My life has never been the same since.

*The beautiful, tiny Teacup Maltese!*

Since you're reading this book, I think it's safe to assume that you, too, are interested in bringing home a new bundle of joy—in which case, congratulations! In my humble opinion, you couldn't have picked a better breed. Or perhaps you've already brought your new Teacup Maltese home but aren't sure what you should do next; trust me, I've been there! Either way, there are several things that you should know about your new dog.

There's so much to learn about this breed. Some I've learned the hard way, through trial and error; other bits of information I've picked up from breeders, vets, fellow Teacup Maltese and Miniature Maltese enthusiasts, and my own research.

To help others like myself, who have an undying love for these dogs and a desire to know everything there is to know about them, I decided to compile this book of information, tips and tricks, and details of my personal experience with these adorable, remarkable animals, all in a personal, easy-to-understand format.

We'll cover all sorts of topics, from Teacup Maltese grooming and Teacup Maltese feeding and nutritional needs to temperament, detailed training methods, and the do's and don'ts of caring for your little angel.

The challenges of owning and caring for a Toy Maltese are significantly different from those associated with most other dogs. Before I bought my first dog, Snowbell, I tried to do a little research on the breed, and boy, I was frustrated with some of the Maltese care books I picked up. None of them were specific to the Toy variety, for such a tiny dog presents unique challenges. I wanted detailed, well-compiled information that applied to the Teacup Maltese, and not just any generic dog. Well, fear not! While a lot of the tips and tricks you'll find later on can indeed apply to most dogs, the focus of this book is the Maltese — and to some extent its mixes, like the Maltipoo.

While my preference for these dogs is just that, a preference, I think it's safe to say that the Miniature Maltese is one of the most popular of the toy breeds, for many reasons that we'll cover together later in the book. If you are indeed thinking about getting one of these dogs, I promise that your life will only improve if you apply these Teacup

Maltese tips and techniques. But, as I'm fond of saying, knowledge is power. Always educate yourself on the breed of your dog before you bring her home, to ensure that both you and your new pet have the smoothest transition possible.

With that being said, thank you ever so much for purchasing this guide, and I hope that it will enrich your life and bring you one step closer to finding the perfect little bundle of energy and love that is the Teacup Maltese.

*Picture time! Teacup Maltese dogs are smart, sweet, and sassy!*

***

## Chapter 2 - Teacup Maltese:
## The Miniature Maltese in History

* * *

Have you ever glanced at your dog and wondered, with genuine interest and curiosity, where your pet came from? One of the things that sparked the idea for this book was me sitting on my porch swing a few months back, drinking a nice cold glass of sweet tea and watching my three Miniature Malteses (Snowbell, my first, and Jasmine and Lily, who are sisters) frolic and play on the front lawn. As I watched them, I began to ponder where they'd come from. My love for Teacup Maltese dogs had grown, and after the joy that that they had brought to my life, I wanted to know absolutely everything about them. Which got me wondering—where did the amazing dog we now know as the Teacup Maltese come from, and for what purpose had they been bred?

*Pretty in pink!*

The Maltese have a completely fascinating history, one that I've been mildly obsessed with. It's fascinating to imagine the ancestors of my pets running around Italy hundreds of years ago, not to mention the people who might have owned them. While this chapter isn't exactly essential to the care of your Miniature Maltese, I think it's a good idea to familiarize yourself with the origin of your dog's breed.

The Toy Maltese, first and foremost, is a slight variation of the regular Maltese, which origins can be traced back nearly 2,500 years (although there's no concrete proof, some claim it's been around for even longer—Charles Darwin, the father of evolutionary theory, placed the breed at about 8,000 years old)! In fact, one of the earliest known examples of Maltese dogs in art was estimated to have been created around 500 B.C.

True to its name, this perky little dog is thought to have originated from the tiny Mediterranean island of Malta, although some people argue that it might have come from the now-nonexistent Sicilian town of Melita. Personally, I think it's more probable that it originated from Malta, but since I don't hold a degree in doggy history, that's just my guess. Either way, the Maltese came from the Mediterranean, I think we can all agree on that.

*The tiny Mediterranean island of Malta, located off the coast of Italy, is the most likely origin of the Maltese breed.*

Many prominent historical figures either owned Maltese dogs or described them in historical documents and fictional pieces. The famed Greek philosopher Aristotle mentioned this dog in some of his writings, and Roman poet Marcus Valerius Martialis wrote several verses about a 'small white dog", and many people believe that he was, in fact, referring to the Maltese.

### Teacup Maltese Terrier, Miniature Maltese Terrier, Bichon Maltese—Why So Many Different Names?

Throughout history, the Maltese have gone by many different names; Bichon Maltese, Maltese Terrier, Spaniel Gentle, Bichon, and the Maltese Lion Dog are just some of the monikers that the Maltese have gone by over the years!

Although 'Maltese' is this dog's official name, some people still choose to call the Maltese by its older names. That's perfectly okay; however, it's important to keep in mind that these names all describe the same dog. My reason for including this subchapter is this. Some breeders will use old and forgotten names for their dogs in order to make them sound more exotic, and therefore charge more for their puppies. But as long as you know that a Maltese Lion Dog is really just a Maltese, you won't get swindled!

One thing worth mentioning, however; don't confuse the Bichon, which is another name for the Maltese, with the Bichon Frise, which is another breed of dog entirely.

### The Evolution of the Maltese Dog

What I find the most interesting, perhaps, is the reason this breed was so popular. You see, historically most dogs were kept for a certain purpose—hunting, vermin control, herding, protection. It wasn't until fairly recently that dogs were considered pets; they all had a job to do, just like people. But for thousands of years, because of their stunning beauty and gentle, easy-going nature, Maltese dogs were popular as pets. They were extremely popular amongst the nobility and upper-class women. It was considered very fashionable to lounge around with a Maltese in one's lap, or to take one of these tiny, adorable dogs along for a stroll around town. Some people considered them an absolute must-have accessory, just like a designer handbag. I can only imagine how expensive they used to be if they were reserved mostly for nobility!

*The long, silky hair of the Teacup Maltese is one of its most notable features and has attracted many admirers.*

In fact, speaking of money, here's another neat fact; Maltese dogs were so prized, they were often used as objects of barter; in other words, money!

Maltese dogs used to be a lot bigger. In the mid-1600's, many breeders decided that the Maltese needed to be much smaller, and began crossing the early Maltese with other toy breeds, shrinking the size and changing many of the characteristics, until eventually, we wound up with the diminutive, gorgeous dog that we have today. Fortunately, with the introduction of kennel clubs, a breed standard for the Maltese was established.

The Teacup Maltese, also known as the Toy Maltese or Miniature Maltese, is a relatively recent breed variation. Only in the past couple of decades have we seen a variation in size. Using selective breeding, regular Maltese dogs that happened to be slightly smaller than the breed standard were bred with other Maltese dogs with similar genes, producing smaller dogs. (we'll cover more about this in the next chapter).

The Maltese have a rich and fascinating history, but their fame hasn't diminished—if anything, they're just as popular today as they were hundreds of years ago.

Tons of famous people have owned Maltese dogs—and the smaller variation, the Teacup Maltese—from Queen Victoria and Marie Antoinette to Elizabeth Taylor and Halle Berry, proving the fact that the Maltese's popularity is indeed timeless!

## Chapter 3 – Teacup Maltese Size And How To Tell A Miniature Maltese From A Standard Maltese

\* \* \*

Without a doubt, it's extremely confusing knowing exactly what to call your new dog. Is it a Toy Maltese or a Miniature Maltese? Is there even a difference between the two? Well, we're going to clear up any confusion.

The only 'official', as in recognized by the American Kennel Club, kind of Maltese is the regular, standard Maltese. According to their standards, a Maltese should weigh about six or seven pounds (or two and a half to three and a half kilograms.)

However, there are variations in size, depending on the bloodline of the dog in question. Dogs that are naturally smaller than their counterparts are selected to breed with other diminutive dogs. Because of this, we now have dogs that are smaller than the breed standard. Miniature Poodles, Teacup Chihuahuas, Miniature Yorkies, and, of course, Teacup Malteses, are all products of selective breeding.

## Adult Maltese--Teacup Maltese Full Grown Size

While 'Teacup' and 'Miniature' are terms that can both be applied to a smaller-than-average dog, typically, a Miniature Maltese would weigh somewhere around the four pound (1.8 kg) range when fully grown, and a Teacup Maltese would weigh less than that—about three pounds (1.4 kg). This is an arbitrary term, however; either word can apply to your tiny Maltese.

*An adorable Teacup Maltese puppy would be the perfect addition to your family!*

Teacup Malteses typically cost more than Standard Malteses. I paid a thousand dollars (£692) for Snowbell, and while my other two were rescues, they would have gone for around the same price on the market had they been sold. The price can range from five hundred dollars all the way up to several thousand dollars (£350 to £1300) depending on the breeder and the bloodline of the dog.

Unfortunately, because Teacup Maltese dogs are in such high demand, the market is often flooded with sickly, inbred, severely underweight dogs that were never cared for properly. Sadly, many people see these dogs as nothing more than a source of income, and it's absolutely heartbreaking.

There are several things you need to watch out for when searching for an ethical breeder, which we'll cover more in detail in later chapters. For now, though, I have a story that might shed some light on this ever-growing problem.

I got my first Miniature Maltese, Snowbell, and as I've said she stole my heart right away. Bursting with pride, I called one of my close friends (we'll call her Sandy, to preserve her anonymity) and invited her to come over and see my new dog.

Sandy was enamored by Snowbell's tiny size and fluffy white fur. As Snowbell yapped and bounded around, Sandy decided on the spot that she was going to get a Miniature Maltese, too. However, she wanted one even smaller than Snowbell (the breeder, who was absolutely excellent I should add, told me that my new puppy should weigh about four pounds at adulthood, and he was right.) She began looking online, and immediately found a breeder that sold Teacup Malteses.

I knew right away that something was off when, at the bottom of the anonymous-looking web page, I saw a section declaring that they were having a sale on puppies "with a limited health guarantee." These Teacup Maltese puppies were half-off, and perfect for Sandy's budget. She decided that she wanted one.

"Sandy," I'd told her, "this doesn't sound right to me. Why would these puppies have a limited health guarantee?"

She simply shrugged her shoulders. "I'll take it to the vet first thing and make sure it's healthy. It'll be okay. I really want one, and I don't have the money to buy one at full price."

I tried to discourage her, but she was determined, and a week later, she invited me over to see her new puppy, whom she'd named Max.

He was absolutely adorable, and tiny too—he could fit in my hand. But something was wrong with him. He didn't bound around and play like Snowbell, but instead crouched fearfully in his basket, as if he'd never been outside of a cage in his life and wasn't sure what to do with his new freedom. He was lethargic and apathetic. Sandy did indeed take him to the vet, and nothing was found to be physically wrong with him.

Nevertheless, within a month he had died. The vet diagnosed the cause of death as a lingering internal infection that had been overlooked in the initial exam. Sandy was absolutely heartbroken. True to the breeder's declaration, they offered Sandy no sort of refund or replacement and took no responsibility for the puppy's death.

I'm not trying to scare you away from getting a Teacup Maltese. There are plenty of people who breed them safely and responsibly. I just want you to be aware of the risks involved if you choose to buy from an anonymous breeder.

I was blessed to find a breeder who genuinely cared for his dogs and made sure that the puppies always found great, loving homes.

Of course, Teacup and Miniature dogs face unique health challenges because of their tiny size, and we'll cover those in detail in later chapters as well.

All in all, I personally prefer Miniature Malteses over regular ones. Who wouldn't love a cute, tiny ball of fluff? And their personalities definitely don't match their size; my three are fearless for such little things, and absolutely bursting with tons of love to give to an attentive, caring owner.

Overview: A Standard Maltese should weigh six to eight pounds (or 2.7 to 3.6 kilograms) and Teacup and Miniature Malteses generally weigh between 3-5 pounds (or 1.4 to 2.3 kilograms) when fully grown.

*Teacup Maltese dogs have definitely mastered the 'puppy-dog eyes'!*

## Chapter 4 – Is The Teacup Maltese the Right Dog For Me? Teacup Maltese Temperament, Teacup Maltese Grooming, and Teacup Maltese Space Needs

***

I t's always an excellent idea to thoroughly research the breed of dog that you're interested in before you go through the process of searching for a breeder and picking out a dog. One reason that nearly 4 million dogs wind up in shelters every year in the United States alone is because people choose a dog that isn't compatible with their personality or lifestyle. It's a tragic situation that can easily be avoided by acquainting yourself beforehand with the type of dog that you want.

*Teacup Maltese dogs may be cute, but they have very specific needs that must be met if you want to own one.*

I volunteer part-time at a local animal shelter, and I've lost count of the number of dogs I've seen that have walked through these doors. Usually, I have a little chat with the owner beforehand, gathering information and asking them what exactly went wrong with their pet. Behavioral problems are the number-one reason that owners choose to part with their pets (in the Training chapter, we'll cover a couple of in-depth training plans designed to eliminate the most common behavioral problems in all dogs, as well as some that are prevalent in the Teacup Maltese). The second most prevalent reason is simply a lack of mutual understanding between the person and the dog.

Every breed is different, and every dog within that breed, additionally, is also different. Two of my Miniature Malteses, Lilly, and Jasmine are sisters born from the same litter. They look exactly the same, but their personalities couldn't be more unique. Therefore, you shouldn't bank on your dog acting exactly like the 'breed standard'. I've encountered lazy hound dogs, aggressive Labradors, and kind, sweet pit bulls. Stereotypes exist in every breed. However, you can usually get a general idea of what to expect by researching the breed.

With the Teacup Maltese, there are several things to consider. Let's break them down.

**Teacup Maltese Space Needs**

Typically, your Teacup Maltese won't need much space, making them perfect for people who live in apartments or condos. It's often said that the smaller the dog, the more suited they are for apartment living. That simply isn't the case. Many toy breeds are too hyperactive and noisy for small, enclosed spaces. However, the Teacup Maltese is the perfect choice for those who live in apartments. They tend to be calm dogs who aren't prone to excess barking, so your neighbors will definitely thank you!

For the most part, there's no need to take them to a dog park or a field to run around and expend that extra energy—two short walks per day ought to do it. Although, if you have a younger dog or a dog that has more of an active streak, a longer walk can't hurt. But since a Teacup Maltese is such a tiny dog, normally they tend to be much calmer than their larger counterparts.

However, this doesn't mean that the Teacup Maltese doesn't like to play! From personal experience, I can honestly say that they are very playful, especially when they're puppies. Make sure you provide them with plenty of toys and, if at all possible, another furry playmate.

### Teacup Maltese Dogs—How Much Attention Do They Need?

Here's where a lot of prospective Teacup Maltese owners run into trouble. It's easy to take a look at one of these tiny, snow-white dogs sitting calmly in their bed or basket and assume that they don't need a whole lot of attention from their owners. This couldn't be further from the truth.

Your Teacup Maltese craves company and attention. Even when they're not in the mood to play or snuggle, they at least like to know that you're nearby. They thrive off of constant love and affection, and if you're not going to be able to provide that, it'd be kinder to consider getting a different dog, one that can handle being alone.

*Your tiny little Teacup Maltese will need tons of love and affection!*

In today's day and age, nearly everyone works. It's unavoidable. However, if you have to go to work every day and still want the comfort and companionship of a Teacup Maltese, there are a few things you can do to ensure that both you and your dog are comfortable and happy.

Separation anxiety is extremely common amongst these dogs, and if left unchecked can become a serious problem. If you plan on bringing home a Teacup Maltese puppy, I'd highly advise you to focus on preventing separation anxiety while they're still young. It's easier to prevent than it is to solve; however, if you have a pup that barks or howls frantically, pees in the house, or obsessively chews your furniture or doorframes when you leave the house, it's not the end of the world; using several proven training methods, you can help your dog remain calm while you're away—and not to mention save your house in the process.

If you're unable to stay home with your Teacup Maltese throughout the day, you might want to consider enrolling your dog into a doggy daycare. Many vets and pet store centers (such as PetSmart in the United States, and Doggies Day Out in the UK), as well as several independently-run businesses, offer this service to people who are unable to be home for their pets during the day. Personally, I highly recommend this option. Your dog will have the opportunity to play and socialize with other dogs (usually dogs are kept in areas with other dogs of their size, so you won't have to worry about your tiny Teacup Maltese getting trampled by a Great Dane). The people watching over your dog are highly trained professionals who will know exactly what to do if a problem arises, and treats and meals are often given at the daycare; you can speak with the supervisors to ensure that your dog's meal plan remains the same.

Just be sure to familiarize yourself with the daycare before you bring your Maltese over for the first time. Talk to other patrons of the daycare, read reviews, and get to know the people who run the facility. If you begin to see discouraging signs, like bad reviews or unsanitary conditions, run. You can always find another one, and the minor inconvenience of looking for another place to help you with your dog is worth the elimination of potentially life-threatening risks to your pup.

However, doggy daycare can quickly become costly. If you work five days a week, you can expect to pay up to five hundred dollars a month (£350), and that's incredibly expensive!

There's a cheaper option if you're looking for ways to keep your Teacup Maltese happy and comfortable while you're gone—dogsitters. There are pros and cons to hiring dogsitters. The best thing is that your dog will remain at home, the place that he or she is most familiar with. Dogsitters are much cheaper than daycares, and you have a greater level of control. Many excellent people would be more than willing to care for your baby while you're away.

However, the downside to hiring a dogsitter is that you're less likely to work with a professional. An ideal dogsitter has lots of prior experience, is trustworthy and patient, and knows at least basic doggy first aid as well as what exactly to do in an emergency situation. It's tempting to pay someone that you know to watch your Teacup Maltese, and that's an excellent idea—as long as the person you have in mind meets all those criteria. You can find a dogsitter that fits your budget, timeline, and needs by browsing https://www.care.com (USA and Canada) or http://www.animalangels.co.uk (UK) which are both great websites for finding babysitters, dogsitters, and housesitters.

Personally, I prefer daycares, for the socialization opportunities that they offer for my pups as well as for the peace of mind, but that's not always an option for everyone. Your Teacup Maltese will be perfectly happy either way— all he wants is love and attention.

## Maltese Temperament — Are They Family-Friendly?

Teacup Malteses are affectionate, playful, calm little dogs that are remarkably adaptable. However, they aren't suited for every family dynamic.

These dogs are so little and delicate, and therefore won't be able to handle small children who might inadvertently play roughly with them. Even if you explain to your child that your Teacup Maltese could get hurt, they don't always understand and could accidently injure your dog. When I first brought home Snowbell, my sister and her husband came over one day to visit. They brought their three-year-old son along. I love my nephew with all my heart, and I explained to him that he had to be gentle with my puppy because she was so tiny. But you can't really expect a toddler to understand, and when he picked her up, he accidently dropped her on the hardwood floor, and Snowbell broke her paw. I was frantic, but even then I understood that it could have been a lot worse. She healed up just fine, and while I knew that it was only an accident, it has to be understood that such tiny dogs and children don't mix. Therefore, if you have a child under the age of five, it isn't wise to get a Teacup Maltese.

They are gentle dogs but still might bite or snap in stressful situations. If you have children, make sure that they understand that rough hugs or constant teasing might result in a painful nip. No matter how gentle and patient your dog is, children shouldn't be left around them unsupervised. It's a precaution that might prevent stress or harm to your dog or your child.

## How Often Do Teacup Maltese Dogs Need To Be Groomed?

This is another reason that many dogs, particularly high-maintenance breeds like the Teacup Maltese, often lose their homes; their owners get them without realizing just how often they need to be groomed. While working at the shelter, I had a Maltipoo come in with a thick, dirty, matted coat. Her owners had been overwhelmed with the amount of care needed for her and hadn't been able to meet those needs. It's heartbreaking, but preventable if you're willing to expend the amount of time, money, and energy needed to maintain these dogs.

*These little fluffy babies need lots of grooming; invest in a good brush and detangling comb.*

The coat of the Teacup Maltese is long, fine, and silky. They rarely shed, and many people consider them hypoallergenic, just like the Poodle. A Teacup Maltese is an excellent choice if you're worried about dander or lots of loose, white dog hairs sticking to your clothes. I rarely spot dog hair on my clothes or furniture.

When it comes to coat length, there're two options you can choose for your Teacup Maltese—natural or short.

Naturally, the Maltese have a long, silky coat that feels just like human hair. And just like human hair, it must be brushed daily. Otherwise, it will tangle and mat. Even if you decide to keep the coat long, it's important to trim the hair along their ears and face. They have to be bathed often in order to maintain the clean coat. A Teacup Maltese is pure white, so their coat is prone to staining; frequent baths are needed to prevent this.

Many people decide to go with a short trim. It's easier to maintain; although, in my opinion, it detracts from the graceful, elegant look that the Maltese are famous for. Even if you opt for trimming your dog's hair short, it's still important to brush and bathe them often.

Either way, consistent grooming is needed for this dog, and that's definitely something to keep in mind if you're considering getting a Teacup Maltese.

**Checklist:**

| Yes | No | Will I be able to spend enough time with my Teacup Maltese? |
|-----|-----|-----|
| Yes | No | If not, will I be able to provide them with the attention that they need while I am away? |
| Yes | No | Does my household consist of adults or older children who will be gentle with my tiny dog? |
| Yes | No | Do I have the space necessary for my Teacup Maltese to remain happy and comfortable? |
| Yes | No | Am I willing to put in the effort to maintaining and caring for my Teacup Maltese's silky coat? |

If you answered "yes" to all of these questions, then you are ready to own a Teacup Maltese!

***

## Chapter 5 – Maltese Puppies For Sale—Buying And Adopting Teacup Maltese Puppies

***

Befgore you rush off to the nearest breeder, first, you should decide if you want a puppy or a full-grown Teacup Maltese.
Both choices have their merits. I prefer getting a puppy, but many people opt for an adult dog.

## Teacup Maltese Puppies For Sale!
## Should I Get a Puppy or an Adult Dog?

Puppies are absolutely adorable, but there are some definite drawbacks to selecting a puppy as opposed to a full-grown dog. They tend to be more expensive, both in outright costs and in vet bills and supplies; not to mention obedience school, any clothing or accessories they might outgrow, etc. Many adult dogs are already housebroken and have at least basic behavioral training. If you get a Teacup Maltese puppy, you must be willing to train it, no matter how frustrating it might be.

There's a common misconception that puppies form a much stronger bond with their new owners than adult dogs do. For some dogs, especially older ones that have passed through the hands of many different people, that is the case, but for the most part that isn't true. If you show your dog love and affection, it will open its heart to you no matter how old it is.

With adult dogs, you already have a clear understanding of their personality and temperament. When you get a puppy, it's usually a surprise, either pleasant or otherwise.

However, it's an absolute joy to raise a puppy and watch it grow from a tiny, frolicking baby into an adult.

*Puppies are cute, but full-grown Teacup Maltese dogs are tiny and adorable too—and they also need love!*

Whether a puppy or full-grown Teacup Maltese would be a better choice for your lifestyle is up to you to decide.

## Maltese Puppies For Adoption and Maltese Rescue

Now, should you buy a dog or adopt one?

In this context, 'adopting' means to choose a dog from an animal shelter or rescue group. Adopting a dog is a more drawn-out and thorough process than simply buying one; you will have to provide a valid form of I.D, proof of residency, and, in some cases, proof of income. Adoption protocol varies in different states, provinces, and countries; for example, in my state dog adoption is relatively straightforward. However, in other states, the process may take up to a week or more and includes house inspection and references. Be sure to familiarize yourself with the adoption protocols in your area before you make plans to adopt a Teacup Maltese.

If you have the opportunity to adopt a Teacup Maltese, definitely do so. I'm a firm believer in rescue; two of my dogs were rescued from an unscrupulous breeder who kept them in a locked cage with five other dogs. I was able to save them from such an awful existence, and I'm so glad I did. However, if you're looking for a specific breed of dog, that opportunity doesn't always present itself.

There are rescue groups that specify in rehoming certain breeds. There are tons of Maltese rescue groups; however, since the Teacup Maltese is such a rare variation, there aren't any to my knowledge that only rescue Teacup Maltese dogs.

You can always check out your local shelters. Many people falsely believe that shelters only offer mutts or sick dogs. Out of all the dogs that are currently in the shelter, I volunteer at, about a fourth of them are purebred. You never know what you might find, and shelters are without a doubt cheaper than buying from a breeder—not to mention most of the time they come already spayed or neutered, as well as vaccinated (be sure to ask beforehand so you have a good understanding of the dog's health and medical history). You'd be supporting a really good cause if you adopted a Teacup Maltese from a shelter!

Additionally, you might find people who already have a Teacup Maltese, who don't want to, or are unable to, care for it anymore due to any number of circumstances. You could offer to take the pup in yourself, and that way you'd be helping both the people and the dog by providing it with a loving home.

**Buying Teacup Maltese Puppies**

If you decide to buy a dog instead, one thing to keep in mind is the cost. Teacup Maltese puppies can cost upwards of a couple thousand dollars, if not more. A dog around the seven-hundred-dollar mark (£480) is ideal, but still, that's a lot of money. It's only yet another reason to make absolutely certain that you're prepared to own a Teacup Maltese.

You might have to begin your search several months in advance in order to find the perfect dog. You can try looking for pet stores, breeders, or people selling dogs through newspaper ads or online classifieds.

I should clarify; you should never, ever buy puppies from people who sell them through classifieds, either online or in print. Most of these people are shady backyard breeders, and you should avoid them at all costs. However, if you come across someone selling a single older dog, a family pet that they can no longer care for, that's an entirely different matter. Although these dogs usually aren't 'sold', they're 'rehomed'.

Pet stores are another option, although I would avoid them as well unless they can provide you with definite proof that their dogs come from good breeders. Many pet stores buy puppies from breeders who mass-produce their dogs in cramped cages, with little to no human interaction and no vet care at all. However, there are plenty of independently-owned pet stores who work with professional, ethical breeders, and usually, they will be more than happy to let you tour their facilities beforehand to ensure that your puppy comes from the best possible background.

**Finding a Good Teacup Maltese Breeder**

Breeders are the best option, hands-down. You can begin your search online; many breeders own a web page or advertise in social media groups. It's best to start local; then, if you are unable to find a suitable breeder, broaden your search. Prepare to travel if necessary; I had to go two states over to find a great breeder when I bought Snowbell.

*Good breeders almost always allow you*
*to meet the puppy's mother.*

Do not, I repeat, DO NOT buy your dog from an anonymous breeder. A person who offers no photographs of their facilities, or who refuses to let you visit to look at the dogs and their living conditions and either ships the puppy to you, or meets you somewhere to hand it over, are most likely running a puppy mill. Puppy mills are such a huge problem, especially for in-demand dogs like the Teacup Maltese. I will be covering puppy mills thoroughly in the next chapter.

Instead, opt for a breeder that shows nothing but the utmost care for their dogs, who is knowledgeable about the breed, and is more than happy to let you visit and look around before you decide to buy.

The best breeders offer puppies that come with a health clearance, meaning that they have been tested and screened for common health problems and that they are free of genetic disorders. Many breeders allow you to meet the mothers to get a good understanding of their health and temperament, as many of the most common issues are genetic.

All in all, both adoption and buying from a breeder are good choices.

## Chapter 6 – Puppy Mills

***

Puppy mills are a global epidemic. Every year in the United States alone, millions of dogs are sold to people who have absolutely no idea where these dogs come from or what their money is supporting.

I decided to include a chapter on puppy mills because Teacup Malteses are often bred in these awful places. But puppy mills are a crime against all dogs, and the only way to put a stop to them is through education and awareness.

**Mini-Maltese—Irresponsible Breeding and Puppy Mills**

Puppy mills are places where dogs are mass-produced in cramped, filthy cages, all with the intention of turning a profit for the breeder. The dogs receive no medical attention, and the puppies are snatched from their mother at the earliest possible moment, to be sold to the unknowing public.

There are an estimated 10,000 puppy mills in existence in the United States alone, and it's estimated that one out of every three dogs sold in the UK come from puppy mills. Few people who know about puppy mills and, unfortunately, even fewer are willing to talk about them. To many people, it's just another dirty little secret to be swept under the rug. It needs to be brought out and discussed. When I attempt to talk to people about puppy mills, I often get shrugged shoulders and statements like, "At least it doesn't happen around here." You'd be shocked to discover that there very well might be a puppy mill in your area. These places aren't advertised, after all.

This disgusting, greedy, profit-driven industry rakes in millions in profits a year, all based on the pain and suffering of innocent animals. Nobody wants his or her money to be added to that staggering amount, and so it's crucial to understand what puppy mills are and what they do.

Most puppy mills consist of a large house or building in which hundreds of dogs, sometimes thousands, are housed together, usually in cages. They're forced to live in a pile of their own feces and urine, and often get very little food or water. They've never smelled fresh air, they've never felt grass under their paws, and they've never known the comfort of a human touch.

*This heartbreaking picture is, sadly, a common sight around the world, and puppy mills will never go away unless we make a stand against them.*

The people who run these places care only for money. The less they spend, the greater the profit; therefore, next to no money gets spent on these dogs. That means no vet visits, no grooming, and cheap, low-quality food when and if they're fed at all.

The breeding mothers are bred during every single heat cycle for their entire lives until they are no longer able to breed. Think of it this way—imagine a human woman who is forced to give birth every single year, from the time she's fifteen until she's sixty-five. That's extremely unhealthy, both for the mother and her babies, and that's the life of a puppy mill breeding dog.

Then, after the mother dog is no longer able to breed, she's put down. Her life only has value when she's giving birth and turning a profit for the owner.

I've volunteered at my local shelter for many years now, and I'm absolutely astounded every time I get wind of a puppy mill bust in my area. My shelter usually volunteers to help with the seizure of the dogs and with rehabilitation, meaning that, whenever puppy mills get shut down within a hundred-mile radius of my shelter, we see hundreds of dogs suffering from various degrees of abuse and neglect.

Less than six months after I started at the shelter, one of my fellow volunteers came rushing toward me in excitement as I pulled into the driveway. "Come on!" she'd exclaimed. "Everyone's getting ready now."

"Getting ready for what?"

"The SPCA shut down a puppy mill operation two counties over. Everyone's gearing up to help them move the dogs out."

This was news to me. Some of the other volunteers filled me in as I joined the rescue team. Apparently, the puppy mill had been in business for over ten years. Until undercover animal-rights agents exposed them, no one had known just how huge of an operation it was, nor the conditions that the dogs were kept in. Nearly every pet store in the state had gotten their dogs from this 'breeder'.

When we arrived, I was absolutely shocked and appalled at what I was seeing. I'd heard of puppy mills, sure, but hearing and seeing were two different things.

An entire barn was filled with dogs. Wire cages meant to house chickens were stacked on top of each other almost to the ceiling, and in each cage were anywhere from five to fifteen dogs. All of them were filthy and barking frantically. Their coats were matted with dirt, and a thick layer of clumped-up feces and urine coated the concrete floor in every direction. The bottoms of the cages were open wire, so many of the dogs had hurt their paws falling through the cage only to be stopped by the crisscrossing wire. The dogs in the bottom cages were absolutely soaked from the pee falling on top of them from the dogs in the upper cages. A lot of the dogs were sick and injured.

I couldn't stand the smell; I pressed my sleeve against my nose, tears filling my eyes, as much as from shock and horror as from the overwhelming stench. One of the SPCA workers passed me a medical mask, but even through it I could barely breathe in that barn.

Many of the dogs were blind. Some weren't moving in their cages at all. These dogs were either dead or so close to death that it didn't really matter.

The man who ran the puppy mill was arrested, and we were left with the daunting task of removing five hundred and eleven dogs from the barn and into a temporary shelter, where they would be assessed by a veterinarian and relocated to shelters all over the state.

We began to unload the dogs from their cages and place them in travel crates. For many of them, it was the first time ever being touched by a human hand. They whimpered and cried and wagged their tails and tried to lick our faces. Every single one of them was crawling with fleas.

They were all pure-bred dogs; Labradors, Chihuahuas, Poodles, Yorkies. And Malteses, of course. At least a fifth of the dogs were Malteses.

As we slowly worked our way through the room, I paused. In a cage at the bottom of a tall stack, cramped in with several other dogs, were two tiny, tiny white puppies. They were yapping at all the noise and confusion. Their pretty coats were matted and soaked, and they looked absolutely miserable. They were severely underweight. These two puppies stole my heart immediately. They were Miniature Malteses, but unlike my own Snowbell, they weren't happy and playful.

When we got back to the temporary shelter with all five hundred dogs in tow, I'd made up my mind to adopt those two puppies. Once they were cleared by the vet, I took them home, cleaned them up, and gave them lots of love. Today they're unrecognizable. Jasmine and Lily were lucky; they were able to get out of that horrible situation. Many dogs don't. Out of the five hundred and eleven dogs, we rescued, eight of them died.

My point is, because Teacup Malteses, and toy dogs in general, are so in-demand, they're extremely likely to come from puppy mills.

The absolute worst part is that puppy mills are legal, as long as nobody knows that the dogs are being neglected — and often these places are hidden from the public eye. If you buy a purebred puppy from a pet store or an anonymous breeder, you run the risk of unknowingly supporting a puppy mill.

If you decide to buy a Teacup Maltese puppy, make sure that you choose a good, responsible breeder. Ask to see the dogs and their living conditions beforehand and get the all-clear from a vet before you decide to purchase the dog. There are plenty of excellent, ethical breeders out there, and by choosing them, you can help make a difference.

***

## Chapter 7 – Miniature Maltese Mixes: The Best Of Both Worlds?

***

In the past thirty or so years, the dog world has been taken over by so-called 'designer breeds'. These are dogs whose parents are two separate breeds, usually popular ones. Some of these designer breeds, or hybrid dogs as they are also called, are more sought-after than their purebred counterparts.

### A Short History of the Teacup Maltese Mix

Mixed-breed dogs are nothing new, of course, but what makes designer dogs special is the amount of time and attention spent in creating them. The parent dogs are both purebred with optimal genes, selected for their temperament and ideal breed characteristics.

The Labradoodle was the first hybrid dog to be purposely bred. In the 1970's, someone had the idea to cross a Standard Poodle with a Labrador to create a new breed of hypoallergenic seeing-eye dogs to provide to disabled people who suffered from dog allergies. In just a few years, the popularity of the breed exploded, and following the Labradoodle craze, new hybrid breeds were popping up everywhere. Nowadays, nearly every breed has been crossed with another to create hybrids.

Some of these dogs, like the Labradoodle, were bred to combine desirable characteristics of two different breeds; others, I'm afraid to say, were mostly created by irresponsible breeders to take advantage of a trendy label and make big bucks, for hybrid breeds can be ridiculously expensive.

The Maltese are no exception. Since it's such a beautiful dog, breeders have crossed them with many different breeds, creating a huge spectrum of designer dogs, all of them with different physical characteristics and personality traits.

You might decide that you want a Teacup Maltese mix instead of a purebred. That's perfectly okay; you just need to be aware of the other breed's temperament and needs, as well as make sure that the puppy you pick out was bred responsibly.

**Note:** Remember, even though Maltese hybrids are expensive, in the eyes of kennel clubs they're still technically 'mutts'; therefore, you won't be able to register them, and you won't be able to enter them in dog shows. However, unless you do want to show your dog, don't let that deter you. Papers don't make a dog, and they shouldn't be overly important to you. All that matters is that you provide a happy, loving home to your dog. Also, be sure that your dog comes from a responsible breeder and not an awful puppy mill.

Let's go over a few of the most popular Maltese mixes; what they'll look like, what size they'll reach at maturity, their expected temperament, and what price range you're looking at for such a dog.

**Maltese Poodle Mix, or Maltipoo**

This is the most popular Maltese mix. It's created by crossing a Maltese with a Toy or Miniature Poodle, resulting in a tiny dog with characteristics of both breeds.

All in all, the Maltipoo is an ideal dog. Like both the Teacup Maltese and the Toy Poodle, it is hypoallergenic, making it absolutely perfect for people who are allergic to dogs. It's highly-intelligent, which in turn makes training a breeze. They're very friendly and love to play. And best of all, they're just so darn cute!

*Maltipoos come in a wide array of sizes and colors!*

Although the characteristics of a cross-bred dog depend on the genes of its parents, generally Maltipoos lose the straight, silky fur of the Maltese, in favor of the slightly curly hair of the Poodle. Likewise, while all Teacup Malteses are pure white, the Maltipoo comes in a variety of colors, with brown, black, and silver being the most common. Their size really depends on the size of the Poodle that the parent Maltese was bred with, but you can usually expect a five-to-eight lb. (2.2-3.5 kg.) adult Maltipoo.

### *Teacup Maltipoo and Miniature Maltipoo*

I decided to include a small subsection on Teacup and Miniature Maltipoos because, due to the sheer variety of Poodle sizes, Maltipoos won't always be as small as the Teacup Maltese.

If you want a Teacup or Miniature Maltipoo, always make sure that the parent Poodle is a Toy Poodle, not a Miniature one. Toy Poodles are smaller than Miniature Poodles, and by choosing a Toy Poodle to breed with a Teacup Maltese, you can ensure that your Maltipoo will be tiny!

A Maltipoo puppy can cost anywhere for three hundred to nine hundred dollars (£200 to over £600), depending on the breeder.

### Maltichon

A Maltichon is a cross between a Maltese and a Bichon Frise. Both of these dogs are cute, popular breeds, and when the two are mixed, the result is simply adorable.

Maltichons are generally light-colored, like white, tan, or cream. They rarely shed, although their coat will need a good bit of brushing to keep in order.

They're extremely friendly, although they are generally low-energy and a little stubborner than a purebred Maltese. They're tiny dogs who usually won't get above seven pounds or three kilograms.

They can cost up to one thousand dollars (almost £700).

**Malchi**

A Malchi is a cross between a Maltese and a Chihuahua.

They come in a variety of colors, with black, white, tan, and cream being the most common. They are tiny and can weigh anywhere from five pounds to ten pounds (or two to four and a half kilograms), depending on the size of the Chihuahua. If a Teacup Chihuahua is mixed with a Teacup Maltese, you can expect an especially tiny dog.

*An absolutely adorable example of the tenacious,*
*highly intelligent Malchi.*

Malchis are smart and sassy! Expect a highly-intelligent, independent dog that will nonetheless love to cuddle and play.

These dogs have the fragile constitution of both the Maltese and the Chihuahua, so make sure that you are particularly careful around them.

A Malchi can cost up to a thousand dollars (£680)

## Maltipom

Now, on to my absolute favorite of the Teacup Maltese mixes—the Maltipom. This designer breed combines my two favorite breeds, the Maltese and the Pomeranian, into one fluffy package.

The Maltipom has the perky ears, face, and general stature of the gorgeous Pomeranian and the flowing coat and easygoing nature of the Maltese.

They are small, generally weighing three to nine pounds, and come in a variety of colors.

These dogs are easygoing and friendly in nature; however, if you do not socialize them and raise them with a firm yet gentle hand, they may develop 'small dog syndrome', which is common in independent and headstrong breeds like the Pomeranian.

Maltipom puppies are in high demand, resulting in a designer breed with a high price tag. If you want one of these perky little puppies, expect to pay up to two thousand dollars (£1300)

## Malteagle

This is one of the more unusual Maltese mixes, but one that is slowly gaining popularity nevertheless: a cross between the Maltese and the Beagle.

The Malteagle has the distinctive color pattern of the Beagle and the silky fur of the Maltese, although it may not be as long as its purebred counterparts.

The Malteagle is extremely loyal, intelligent, playful, and loving, and many people think that it truly is the absolute best of the Maltese mixes.

Expect an active dog that loves to play and run. Unlike the other Maltese designer breeds that I've mentioned so far, the Malteagle is not a toy dog. It can weigh up to twenty-two pounds, or ten kilograms when fully grown. One of its parents is a hound, meaning that it will most likely inherit at least some of the Beagle's energy and wanderlust. Make sure to exercise your Malteagle regularly and give it lots of room to run.

Like the Beagle, they are also super-friendly but do tend to have a stubborn streak, so training might be a bit of a challenge.

Unfortunately, due to the incredible rarity of the Malteagle, I couldn't find any information on the general cost of a Malteagle puppy. If you're interested in one, I suggest calling upon a trusted breeder to give you more information on breeders who may currently have some for sale.

**Mauxie**

The Mauxie is a cross between a Maltese and a Dachshund.

These dogs are absolutely adorable and will most likely
have the black-and-tan coloration that is the most common
amongst Dachshunds, although it might also be tan or
dapple. Its coat really depends on what sort of Dachshund
the Maltese it is bred with—smooth, wire, or long-haired.
Most Mauxies have soft, curly hair that will require a daily
brushing.

They will usually inherit the body structure of a Maltese,
losing the trademark long, low-slung body of the
Dachshund.

Mauxies generally weigh four to eight pounds or 1.8 to 3.6
kilograms. Despite their small size, however, they are
tenacious little things that love to run and dig. Be sure that,
if you decide to let them run around, your yard has a
sturdy fence that they can't dig underneath.

They are intelligent and friendly; however, the Maltese and
the Dachshund are both notoriously hard to housetrain, so
if you decide to get a Mauxie make sure that you have the
time and energy needed to housebreak these headstrong
little dogs.

Mauxie puppies generally cost three hundred to eight
hundred dollars (£200 to £550).

**Overview**

These are but a few of the Maltese designer breeds; if I were
to list them all, this little book would turn into a novel.
Every Maltese mix has pros and cons, and every dog is also

different; I'm only trying to give you a general idea of what to expect.

Always make sure that the dog you're interested in is bred responsibly; puppy mills are chock-full of designer breeds. A good idea would be to keep an eye on your local shelter; many mixed breeds wind up in shelters, and one of them might just be the mix you're looking for. The background and health of shelter dogs are questionable, but you'd save a lot of money by adopting such a dog—not to mention you'd be doing an incredibly good deed.

I'm a huge fan of the Teacup Maltese (obviously!), but its mixes can often deliver the best of both worlds.

## Chapter 8 – Your New Teacup Maltese Puppy—How To Make Him Happy and Comfortable

\*\*\*

W hen you first bring your new Teacup Maltese home, it might be easy to get swept up in the excitement. But you have to remember that this is all new for him, and he's scared. He's tiny, after all, and he's in a brand-new environment.

By making preparations and planning out the first 24 hours of your Teacup Maltese's new life, you can ease his transition and help him feel comfortable and safe in your home.

*Teacup Maltese puppies are a bundle of joy,*
*but they need lots of care in the first stages of their lives.*

## Maltese Teacup Puppies — Preparing For The Big Day

If there's more than one person in your household, it's wise to hold a family meeting before getting your puppy. If you have children, explain what a huge responsibility it is to care for a new puppy, especially such a tiny Teacup Maltese, which will require special care and attention.

As long as your children are old enough to understand how fragile a Teacup Maltese is, I think it's a great idea to involve them as much as possible in the upbringing of your new pup.

Make sure that you have a clear idea who will be in charge of scheduling your puppy's life. Who will take the puppy for walks, or out to the backyard to do its business? Who will be in charge of feeding the dog? (Remember, a puppy has to be fed three or four times, if not more, a day). Who will be able to make vet appointments and transport the dog to and from the vet's office? You should expect to take your puppy to the vet often in the first year of its life, for vaccinations, medicine, growth progress, spay and neuter surgeries, etc.

Now's the time to go shopping and purchase everything that your new Teacup Maltese puppy will need.

**Food and Water Bowls**

Make sure you always opt for a stainless steel or ceramic bowl. Plastic bowls are cheaper, but lower-quality. Not only do they tend to break, splinter, or wear down, sometimes chemicals in the plastic can leak into your puppy's food.

Personally, I prefer stainless steel, as it's easy to rinse out and keep clean; however, ceramic is a good option and often comes in many different stylish colors and designs.

Raised dog bowls are another option. These are bowls that are lifted up off the ground. They're good for the dog's posture and digestion; however, they're expensive, and I have yet to find one that's the right size for a Teacup Maltese.

Either way, avoid plastic—that's a rule of thumb that

applies to any and all dog supplies.

### Teacup Puppies—The Best Toys For a Tiny Dog

One of the challenges of owning such a tiny dog is finding a toy that is suited for them. Even some of the toys meant for small breeds are too big for a Teacup Maltese's tiny mouth. That doesn't mean he won't try to play with them anyway; however, you want to make sure your puppy has a toy that's suited for his size.

Small rope toys and miniature tennis balls are my dogs' favorites. Small stuffed toys are also a good choice—just make sure they're doggy-safe. Don't give them a stuffed animal meant for human children; buttons, plastic eyes, and bits of fabric could be chewed off and swallowed, potentially harming your puppy.

Miniature Malteses aren't known to have a real tendency to chew, but all puppies chew to some degree, especially when they're teething. Provide them with a safe, non-toxic rubber chewing toy, which will cut down on ruined shoes and furniture.

Never, ever give your Teacup Maltese rawhide. It's not a toy, as many people think. The dog sees it as food and food only, and will, therefore, eat it instead of playing with it. There're two different schools of thought on rawhide— some say it's safe, others say it's deadly for dogs. In my experience, larger dogs seem to have a better time digesting chewed-up pieces of rawhide than smaller ones. Therefore, you should never give your Teacup Maltese rawhide if you want to avoid blocked digestive tracts, choking, or other potentially fatal health risks.

**Maltese Grooming Supplies**

Make sure you have everything you need to keep your new Teacup Maltese properly groomed. Remember, these are high-maintenance dogs as far as grooming is concerned. You will need to pick up a good detangling comb, a doggy brush, nail clippers (make sure you get one with a nail guard, so you don't cut the quick of the nail, which is an extremely painful and stressful experience for your puppy), a pair of small scissors, and a good doggy shampoo. I like shampoos that are oatmeal-based, as they usually smell really nice and are very gentle on the dog's skin. There are many, many other supplies that you might want to pick up, but these are the absolute basics.

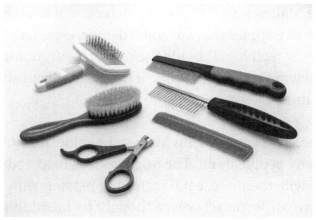

*Basic grooming supplies that you will need to care for your Teacup Maltese: detangling combs, de-shedding brushes, and nail clippers.*

## Bedding

Where is your new Teacup Maltese going to sleep?

It may be tempting to let your dog sleep in the bed with you; however, all in all, a dog bed or a crate is the best option. It helps to set boundaries between you and your dog. But most importantly, the Teacup Maltese is so tiny that, if it were to get restless and jump off your bed, it could injure itself. So it's a wise idea to keep the bed and other high surfaces off limits.

You can purchase an excellent, high-quality bed or a crate either online or at your nearest pet supply store.

## Baby Maltese--Miscellaneous Items

A collar and identification tag are probably the most important things you will ever buy your dog. If he gets outside and gets lost, the ID tag on his collar can help bring him home. I also recommend getting him microchipped at the vet. While we're on the subject of microchipping, let's explore that a bit, as it's an important topic.

Microchipping is a relatively painless procedure in which a tiny chip, about the size of a grain of rice, is inserted underneath your dog's skin. To a dog, it feels about the same as getting a shot. This microchip is then registered with your contact information—name, address, and phone number. If your Teacup Maltese gets lost and someone brings him to the vet or animal shelter, they will scan him for the chip and will be able to find out how to contact you.

Worldwide, millions of pets every year are safely reunited with their owners thanks to microchips; therefore, it's an incredibly good idea to get your Teacup Maltese microchipped. In fact, in the UK, it is mandatory for dog owners to get their dog microchipped.

If you decide to walk your Teacup Maltese (since they're low-energy dogs, many people prefer just to let them outside to do their business, or purchase puppy pads, which are special absorbent training pads that contain attractants that encourage dogs to use the bathroom, for them to use) it's important to get him a leash and a harness as well. A harness is much better than a collar when it comes to being attached to a leash; a harness won't choke them if they become overenthusiastic and strain at the leash.

If your house has stairs, especially ones leading down to a basement, it's a good idea to get a gate to keep your Teacup Maltese from wandering into potentially dangerous parts of the house.

If you have carpet, pick up a good pet odor neutralizing spray. Teacup Malteses are notoriously hard to housetrain (we'll cover more on this in later chapters), and you can expect several accidents from your new puppy.

If you're concerned about costs, you can find many of these things wholesale online. One of the benefits of pre-puppy shopping is that you have time to assemble everything beforehand, instead of sprinting to the pet store with your new pup in tow.

**Boutique Teacup Puppies--Puppy-Proofing**

The next step is to puppy-proof your house. Remember, puppies are babies, and just like babies, they will get into everything imaginable without realizing that they could hurt themselves. It's up to you to make your Teacup Maltese puppy's new home safe.

If you have any loose electrical cords, tape them to the floor or baseboards, or hide them under rugs. All cleaning supplies, household chemicals, batteries, houseplants, and any object that might hurt the puppy if he chews it, should be placed on a high shelf out of reach.

Any objects that are breakable should also be removed, as your pup might knock them down while he's playing. Protecting your home as well as your puppy is important.

Take the time now to install the gate, get his bed in place, and decide where his feeding dish and water bowl should be placed.

When you're through, crouch down and examine your home from a puppy's point of view. If you see nothing that might be dangerous to him, then your home is now ready for your puppy.

If you have any children, you should speak with them once more to lay down ground rules—don't overwhelm your puppy with attention on the first day, and don't fight over who gets to hold him; this will only add stress to an already stressful situation. Make sure that they know to speak softly and calmly around the puppy until he gets used to his new family.

Congratulations, you're now ready to bring your new puppy home!

When you speak to the breeder or previous owner, ask them what the puppy was fed and what sort of schedule he was on. Try to follow that same feeding schedule for the first few days. If you decide to switch his brand of food, do so gradually to avoid digestive problems.

Resist the temptation to let your family hold the puppy in their laps on the drive home; bring a travel crate with you, and place a blanket in the crate.

When you arrive home, it's important to limit your puppy. Everything's new, and he's excited and scared. Limit him to one room at first, and keep it quiet for the first couple of hours. Gradually, let him explore the entire house, one room at a time, to ease his transition.

Teacup Malteses are notoriously adaptable dogs, and in a surprisingly short amount of time your puppy will adapt to his environment and acquaint himself with his new, loving family—even if that family is just you!

## Chapter 9 – Maltese Food—Your Teacup Maltese's Nutritional Needs

***

There're so many different dog food choices out there, it may be hard to decide what to feed your Teacup Maltese. The dog food industry is rampant with unethical and questionable practices, such as using tainted food from underdeveloped countries in order to cut costs. You wouldn't want to feed something like that to your pampered little Teacup Maltese!

Don't worry; as long as you avoid cheap, low-quality supermarket foods, your dog will be fine.

A Teacup Maltese has unique nutritional requirements that must be met if he is to remain healthy and happy.

The good thing about owning a Miniature Maltese is that they are such tiny dogs, they don't eat very much. That's a big bonus because high-quality dog food can get really expensive.

An adult Teacup Maltese will eat anywhere for 150-200 calories a day, depending on its size and energy levels; a hyperactive dog will, of course, eat more than a lazy one.

To maintain your Teacup Maltese's optimum health, every day they need a certain percentage of the following:

## Protein

Protein is crucial for all toy breeds, especially a Teacup Maltese. These little dogs don't need much exercise, with the result that the Maltese, in general, is a breed extremely prone to weight gain. If you choose a dog food that has a higher protein percentage, you can help control your dog's weight.

You might be tempted to simply let them eat what, and when, they want; chubby dogs are cute, and what's a little extra weight, after all? It's not a big deal for a human, but it is for a dog, especially a little one. Their delicate bone structure simply can't handle the extra weight. Therefore, it's extremely important to maintain and control their body weight.

You can check to see if your dog is overweight by feeling their ribs. If you can't feel each individual rib, then it's a good idea to change his diet.

Choose a dog food with a protein content of at least 25 percent.

## Carbs

Just like humans, it's wise to avoid feeding your Teacup Maltese excess carbs in order to maintain a healthy weight.

Some commercial dog foods contain sugar and maple syrup, to add color and flavor. Corn meal, with its high carb content, is just as bad—and it's the main ingredient in many big-name dog food brands. You should always check the ingredients of any food you give your dog to make sure you're not feeding him this fattening, low-nutrient food.

### *Fats*

One of the most endearing qualities of a Teacup Maltese is their long, straight, silky hair. This coat takes a lot of work to maintain however; you can improve the quality of your dog's hair simply by feeding him a diet with plenty of healthy fats, like Omega-3.

One thing you have to look out for is hypoglycemia, also known as low blood sugar. Teacup Malteses are naturally more prone to developing hypoglycemia than other dogs. If you feed him regularly and provide him with a healthy balanced diet, you can avoid this potentially life-threatening disease.

When deciding what type of food to feed your dog, there's generally three options; dry, canned, or homemade.

## Dry Food

*A high-quality, easily chewable dry dog food is
the best choice for your Teacup Maltese.*

If you opt for dry food, never buy it from a supermarket;
always go to your local pet store. They have a much bigger
selection of high-quality dog food. Select a brand that
doesn't contain fillers or additives, and make sure that the
food is small enough for your little dog to chew. It's a good
idea to ask your veterinarian for a brand recommendation;
they usually have a good idea of what food is best suited to
your Teacup Maltese's needs.

Unlike canned food, it's recommended to leave dry food
out for your dog at all times. Many small dogs are nibblers
and will take a bite or two at a time throughout the day.

## Canned Food

Many dogs prefer canned food over dry food. Choose food that is nutritionally complete and separate the food into two meals; one in the morning and one at night. However, it's still important to leave a little dry food out during the day so your dog can snack if he gets hungry, thus lowering his chances of developing hypoglycemia. Control the portions so there's no danger of your dog gaining too much weight.

## Homemade Food

If you're not happy with the dog foods available for purchase, or if you're looking for a healthier, sometimes cheaper option, you might want to consider making your own dog food.

There are so many benefits to homemade food. You can make it in bulk and freeze the extra portions to save time. You know exactly where your dog's meal is coming from. You know without a doubt that it's being made with fresh, high-quality ingredients. And I've never met a dog that didn't prefer homemade food, hands-down, over store-bought food.

There are tons of recipes for delicious, nutritious homemade dog food. You can ask your vet for ideas, or you can find some recipes online. As long as you know what your dog needs, you can come up with your own recipe. There are so many different variations and combinations you can try. Your Teacup Maltese will like the variety!

First, you need to decide on a meat base. There are many low-cost options to choose from, like beef liver, chicken, or pork. Just make sure that whatever protein you choose is free of bones that your dog might choke on.

Contrary to popular belief, dogs need vegetables. Many dogs like carrots, green beans, sweet potatoes, and squash. Incorporate one or more of these into your Teacup Maltese's food.

As a general rule of thumb, dogs don't need much starches or dairy. You can add a spoonful of cottage cheese or some cooked white rice into the food, and that will meet their dietary requirements.

Your homemade dog food should roughly consist of: 60-80 percent meat, 20-30 percent vegetables, up to 10 percent carbs and starches, and up to 5 percent fruits/nuts.

Always make sure you thoroughly wash your dog's bowl after feeding to avoid contamination.

*When in doubt, go natural!*

## Maltese Puppy Treats

As an animal shelter volunteer, I'm often approached by first-time dog owners who have a seemingly endless stream of questions regarding what they should feed their new pup. One question that almost always comes up is treats. What is the best treat for a small dog? Is there a difference between the different types of store-bought treats?

For a tiny dog like the Teacup Maltese, treats aren't a simple matter. You need to choose a treat that is high in protein and low on preservatives because unfortunately most commercial dog treats are chock-full of fillers and preservatives. You also need to make sure that the treat is small and soft enough for them to chew. As mentioned earlier, steer clear of rawhide!

The best store-bought treat I've found so far are the meat-based 'jerky' treats. These tend to be a bit more expensive than corn and flour-based treats, but they're packed with protein and are often coated in a flavorful vitamin paste. Just make sure you break the treat up in pieces small enough for your Teacup Maltese to eat.

**Caution:**

Unlike the bigger, hardier breeds, Teacup Malteses have delicate digestive systems that can't stand up to a lot of junk food and harmful chemicals. They can easily become ill if fed table scraps, so never feed them table scraps. Make sure that your homemade dog food is nutritionally balanced and that every ingredient going into its food is safe for dogs.

**Foods To Avoid**

Never, ever feed your Teacup Maltese any of the following:

- Alcohol
- Apple Seeds—The casing around apple seeds contains trace amounts of cyanide. While it takes a lot of apple seeds to poison a person, for a tiny little Teacup Maltese, just a few could potentially make them very sick. If you choose to add apples to your dog's diet, make sure they are thoroughly cored, and the seeds are removed.
- Avocados
- Chocolate
- Coffee
- Macadamia nuts

- Onions and chives
- Garlic
- Raisins and grapes
- Rhubarb

All of these foods are harmful or potentially fatal to your Teacup Maltese if consumed.

## Chapter 10 – Teacup Maltese Health

***

**E**very breed of dog is more or less susceptible to certain health problems than other dogs. The Teacup Maltese is no exception. They are generally hardy dogs, but they are more likely to develop certain diseases or conditions, which you'll definitely have to keep an eye out for.

Genetics play a huge role in the health of your dog. My first dog, Snowbell, has always had a strong constitution because she comes from a generally healthy bloodline. However, my other two, whose background is questionable at best, often get sick. When you get your Teacup Maltese, always be sure to select one that comes from healthy parents. Your bank account will thank you; vet bills can be extremely costly.

It's crucial to find a vet in your area that both you and your Teacup Maltese are comfortable with, and build a relationship with that vet. She will be responsible for healing your little dog when he's sick or injured, and the better she knows your Teacup Maltese, the more she'll be able to do for him.

*Your Teacup Maltese may be your best friend,*
*but the veterinarian should be his!*

Let's go over some of the most prevalent health risks to Teacup Maltese dogs.

**Micro Maltese—Injury is the Biggest Threat**

The number-one threat to your Teacup Maltese's health and well-being is an injury.

One of the duties that I undertake as an animal shelter volunteer is to communicate frequently with our local vet. I stop by at least once a day to pick up medicine, transport hurt or sick animals to and from the clinic, and get a general idea of what's happening with the animals in our community. And one of the things I see the most, out of all the dogs coming and going from the vet, are tiny dogs that have gotten injured. Tragically, many of them have died.

Toy dogs, such as your Teacup Maltese, are living in a world that is simply too big for them. Every day they take risks and face threats that are minor for a large dog, but potentially life-threatening for a four-pound pup.

It's easy to overlook potential threats, but you should always be vigilant in protecting your dog from harm.

The most common injury in Teacup Maltese dogs is broken bones, which they can sustain from jumping or falling from furniture. To prevent this, you should always give your dog his or her own space. Provide them with a doggy bed, a crate, or a large comfortable pillow or blanket to lounge on during the day. If you decide to bring them onto a chair or couch, always hold them on your lap and never allow them to jump down on their own.

Teacup Maltese dogs like many small dogs, often like to follow you around; and because they're so small, they can be easy to overlook. This may cause them to be stepped on. Be extremely careful when your Teacup Maltese is underfoot; if you step on them, they can be badly injured.

Always supervise your Teacup Maltese when he or she is eating or playing. They can choke on the tiniest object; a single piece of chewed-up plastic or bone splinter can spell death for your dog. When it comes to toxic objects or substances, it only takes a little bit for them to overdose.

Because of their tiny size, if you allow them to play in the yard unsupervised they can easily slip through a gap in the fence and run into traffic.

Like all small dogs, your Teacup Maltese will most likely think he's much bigger than he really is and might pick a fight with a larger dog. Only one bite from a big dog could be fatal.

I'm not trying to scare you with all these scenarios, but it's important for you to be on your guard, just like you would with a baby.

As long as you remain vigilant in your efforts to watch your dog and control his environment, you should be able to reduce his chances of injury drastically.

When it comes to diseases and ailments, there are several that are prominent in the Maltese breed in general, and a few that are most common in the Miniature and Teacup variety. While your first step in treating these disorders should always be to contact your vet , some of them respond well to natural herbal treatments, home remedies, or over-the-counter medications; just make sure that your vet gives you the green light before you administer any medication or treatments to your Teacup Maltese.

**Heart Disease**

Cardiovascular disease is a common ailment in Teacup Maltese dogs, especially senior dogs and dogs with a family history of heart disease. There are many different types of heart disease, ranging from mild to extremely severe.

Here are some common symptoms of heart disease in dogs.

If your Teacup Maltese develops one or more of these symptoms, schedule an appointment with your vet immediately:

- Coughing—Dogs often develop coughs just as people do. Usually, it's nothing to worry about, but if your dog's cough lasts more than three days, contact your vet. It could be a sign of heart disease or another serious condition.
- Breathing difficulty
- Extreme behavioral changes—a sudden lack of energy, loss of interest in companionship or toys, and withdrawing from loved ones are all examples.
- Loss of appetite
- Weight loss or gain
- Fainting
- Weakness or fatigue
- Restlessness

**Eye Problems**

Several eye disorders are common amongst Teacup Malteses.

Corneal ulcer —If your dog suffers a wound in his eye, or if a foreign object becomes trapped underneath his eyelid, a corneal ulcer could form. This disease affects deep layers of the cornea and may become serious. Symptoms include inflamed or watery eyes, squinting, light sensitivity, discharge, or a forming of a film over the eye. Your vet may recommend surgery.

Glaucoma—This is a potentially very serious disease that is

prevalent amongst Teacup Maltese dogs and toy dogs in general. Glaucoma is caused by inadequate fluid drainage in the eye. If left untreated, it could render your dog permanently blind. Symptoms include dilated pupil, frequent blinking, and vision loss.

Progressive Retinal Atrophy—PRA is one of those nasty genetic diseases that is extremely common amongst puppy-mill dogs and dogs that were poorly bred. Most good breeders will be able to show you evidence that all their dogs have been tested for PRA, reducing the chances that your puppy will develop it. PRA causes the rods in the eyes, both eyes, to die, causing permanent blindness. There is no cure; however, if detected early enough, your vet can give you a certain herbal supplement that can slow down the rate of rod decay, thus preserving your dog's sight for as long as possible.

**White Shaker Dog Syndrome**

This is a neurological disease that will cause your Teacup Maltese's entire body to shake. Many times this disorder is mistaken for anxiety, fear, or a chill. If you notice your dog trembling often, it may be White Shaker Dog Syndrome. Your vet might be able to treat it, depending on how severe the case is with your dog.

**Less Serious Ailments**

*Mange:*
Mange is a highly bothersome skin condition that affects dogs of all shapes and sizes; however, due to the Teacup Maltese's delicate constitution, they are highly likely to

contract mange if exposed to infected dogs. There are two types of mange, both caused by tiny parasites. The symptoms of mange include extreme hair loss, skin lesions, and bad odor.

*Fleas:*
Fleas are an absolute nuisance, and every dog owner dreads the sight of the little parasites. Fleas can make your dog extremely itchy and uncomfortable and, if left unchecked, can infest your home. With long-haired dogs such as the Teacup Maltese, fleas can be hard to get rid of; therefore, it's best to prevent them before they become a problem. There're several flea-and-tick prevention medications available through your local veterinarian; these medicines will kill the fleas and ticks that might already be on your dog as well as repel them for a month or more, depending on the medicine. If you don't have access to the medication, you can kill the fleas with a flea-killing shampoo; you can also use Dawn dishwashing liquid, which is safe for dogs and kills fleas on contact (just be sure to avoid getting it in your dog's eyes!)

*Oral Problems:*
Teacup Malteses are prone to mouth and tooth problems such as gingivitis, plaque, inflamed gums, cavities, and tooth decay. Make sure you brush your dog's teeth at least two to three times a week and schedule regular teeth cleaning appointments with your vet.

# A Word About Vaccines

If there's one thing you must do in order to protect your little Teacup Maltese from life-threatening illnesses, it's to be diligent in making sure that he's always up to date on his vaccines. The diseases I listed are only a handful of the ones that your dog might contract. Many, many different diseases are potentially fatal; however, they can be prevented with vaccines.

If you're wondering when you should vaccinate your Teacup Maltese puppy, and for what disease, take a look at this table.

| | |
|---|---|
| 6-7 Weeks | Distemper, Hepatitis, Parvovirus, Parainfluenza, Coronavirus |
| 9 Weeks | Distemper, Hepatitis, Parvovirus, Parainfluenza, Coronavirus |
| 12 Weeks | Distemper, Hepatitis, Parvovirus, Parainfluenza, Coronavirus, Lyme disease |
| 12-16 Weeks | Rabies |
| 16 Weeks | Distemper, Hepatitis, Parvovirus, Parainfluenza, Coronavirus |

This table should just give you a general idea of what to expect. Your vet may decide on a different schedule depending on your Teacup Maltese's health and needs. Frequent vet visits can become expensive, but it'll be worth it, in the long run, to keep your pup safe.

## Chapter 11 – Teacup Maltese Training

O h, boy. So your new pup refuses to use his puppy pad, is aggressive towards other dogs, absolutely hates the leash, or won't come when he's called. Before you start tearing your hair out in frustration, it's important to collect yourself and decide on a detailed training plan.

All Maltese dogs, Teacup and otherwise, are generally receptive to training and eager to please. However, every dog has his own personality, and you might find that your Teacup Maltese is a little stubborner and headstrong than you'd expected. Never fear; it may be a challenge, but you can train him.

### Training Maltese—A Foreword

First things first: always keep in mind that training has nothing to do with intelligence. If your dog doesn't immediately catch on to what you're trying to teach him, it doesn't mean he's dumb. Ultimately, he's an animal—and, if he's a puppy, a baby one at that. Animals think differently than we do, and in order to successfully train them, we have to see things from their point of view.

*Practice makes perfect! Always remain calm and persistent in your Teacup Maltese's training regime.*

Never yell at your Teacup Maltese, even when he's done something 'bad.' Raised voices and angry gestures will only frighten and confuse him. Instead, use positive reinforcement and negative reinforcement.

When he does something right, praise him and give him a treat. Positive reinforcement goes a long way to correcting unwanted behaviors.

Negative reinforcement can also be useful if you be sure to use it in moderation. Never, ever strike your dog, even if it's simply a whack with a newspaper. Likewise, the 'tried and true' method of rubbing a dog's nose in his excrement when he uses the bathroom inside is also extremely cruel. Would you do that to your child if he or she had an accident in the house, as children sometimes do? Of course not, right?

Instead, ignore him. Don't give him praise, don't talk to him, don't even look at him, for half an hour. This has a much more lasting effect on your dog, one that isn't based on fear or intimidation. Dogs, by nature, live for praise and to please their humans. If you pretend he doesn't even exist, he'll definitely get the message.

You should begin your Teacup Maltese puppy's training as soon as possible.

We'll cover two different programs that will target a couple of the most common behavioral problems in this breed—housetraining and aggression.

**White Teacup Maltese--Housetraining**

Here's where a lot of Teacup Maltese owners run into trouble. The Maltese breed in general, while easygoing in most other aspects, is notoriously difficult to housetrain. You might feel on the verge of giving up after countless accidents in the house and be tempted to put your dog outside for good, but please don't. The best place for your tiny pup is inside, where he's safest. Just persevere with this training plan and soon you'll have the bragging rights for a perfectly housebroken Teacup Maltese!

Before you begin: When you first start the housetraining process (preferably when you bring your new dog home for the first time) if possible first remove any rugs or mats.

Dogs instinctively do their business on these, and you'll save yourself a lot of headaches (and scrubbing) if you put these away until your dog is completely trained.

To housebreak your Teacup Maltese, you will have to employ three of the best housetraining methods: paper or puppy pad training, crate training, and outdoors training.

Before you begin, there are several guidelines you need to follow to ensure your pup stays on the right path.

- Control his diet. If his food intake is carefully monitored, soon his digestive system will regulate itself, and he'll adjust to his new schedule.
- Make sure your dog sticks to a schedule; feedings, bedtime, walks, and trips outside should all take place at the same time every day.
- Exercise your pup regularly.

*Crate Training*

You might hate the idea of confining your new puppy in a crate, and your dog might hate it at first too—but crates are one of the most invaluable housebreaking tools available.

There are also many other reasons why it's a good idea to get your dog accustomed to a crate—it makes travel and vet visits much easier if your dog is already comfortable in his crate.

After your puppy gets used to the idea of a crate, he will soon learn to love it. Dogs by nature like to have a place to go when they want to unwind and relax, and as long as you don't confine your puppy inside his crate for too long, to the point that he begins to view it as a prison, he will like it.

The reason that crates are such powerful housebreaking tools is that dogs are clean animals by nature and won't like pee or poop in their living spaces any more than people do. When they feel the urge to go, they will scratch and whine to be let out. Make sure to take them out of their crate right away to use the bathroom; otherwise, they'll learn to think that it's okay to go ahead and go to the bathroom in their crate, and they can use it in your house, too.

### Puppy pads/Newspapers

After you take your pup out of his crate, place him on a puppy pad or newspaper, whichever you prefer—puppy pads, which are special absorbent training pads that can be found for sale at most pet stores or grocery stores, absorb urine much better than newspaper, plus they contain natural attractants that will encourage your dog to go, but they can get expensive quick—and odds are he'll use it right away. Then you put him back in his crate, and after a while, he'll associate using the bathroom with puppy pads or newspapers.

### Outside Training

Since Teacup Malteses aren't dogs that require a lot of outdoor exercise, many people opt to skip this step and simply let them use puppy pads. However, I think it's optimal that you teach them to go outside if it's possible.

Take him outside as frequently as possible, and praise him when he uses the bathroom. Eventually, he will catch on.

If you want to take it a step further, place a puppy pad beside the front door. If your dog is already pad trained, he will immediately run towards the pad when he has to use the bathroom; but before he can, pick him up and take him outside. He'll make the connection between the puppy pad, its position beside the door, and the fact that he needs to pee outside from now on.

Don't give up on your dog. Be extremely diligent; you can't break away from his schedule. Otherwise it's back to square one. It should only take a few weeks for your dog to be completely housebroken.

## Aggression

*He may be tiny, but those teeth can really hurt!*

The good news about Teacup Maltese dogs is that they aren't inherently aggressive; for the most part, they're friendly and easygoing in nature. However, small dogs, in general, have the tendency to become jealous and possibly snappish if not raised with a firm, yet gentle hand. And all dogs can become territorial and mean towards other dogs if they aren't socialized. It's important to begin training your dog to be gentle and friendly.

## Aggression Towards Other Dogs

This is the most common sort of aggression that Teacup Malteses are likely to exhibit an intolerance towards other dogs. He may bark and go crazy when he sees another canine. This occurs when your dog isn't socialized.

The last thing you want is for your tiny Teacup Maltese to run up to a much larger dog and antagonize it; that's a recipe for disaster. Dogs will be dogs, and it wouldn't be the other dog's fault if it snapped at your dog and hurt, or even killed him. As people, it's up to us to eliminate unwanted behaviors in our pets before they become a problem.

You can correct your Teacup Maltese's aggression by bringing him in close proximity to other dogs often, always in controlled situations (make sure both dogs are leashed and the other dog is socialized). Whenever your Teacup Maltese sees another dog, give him praise and a treat (never, ever punish him for his behavior). Soon, he will begin to associate other dogs with good things.

How long it will take to socialize your Teacup Maltese really depends on the dog's personality; some warm up to members of their own species rather quickly, while others need lots of coaxing to become sociable. However, with consistent training, your Teacup Maltese will soon get used to being around members of his own species.

## Aggression Towards People

This isn't as common as dog-against-dog aggression, but it still happens, especially if your Teacup Maltese isn't used to other people. He might bark when someone comes into your home and try to bite them. While your tiny little Teacup Maltese can't do serious damage to a person, people-aggressive dogs are more of a danger to themselves than to people, for the most part. An unfortunate situation involving your Teacup Maltese and another person could end with a lawsuit and forced euthanasia of your Teacup Maltese. I can't imagine how heartbreaking it would be to lose one of my pets in such a manner.

Fortunately, if your Teacup Maltese is territorial and aggressive towards people, you can fix his behavior. However, it's extremely important to understand why your dog acts this way so you can eliminate the problem.

Aggression is an almost entirely fear-based behavior. You should always keep that in mind. Your dog tries to bite people because he is scared or angry—and anger, might I add, is born from fear. For this reason, negative reinforcement won't work, not when it comes to solving the deep-rooted reason for your dog's aggression.

Desensitize him by bringing him into contact with all sorts of people. Some dogs are only aggressive towards women, or large men, or people of different races and backgrounds than the people he lives with. If you push the boundaries of his comfort zone, he will eventually lose his fear.

Take him to parks and on walks throughout the neighborhood; always on a leash, for his own protection. This will introduce him to new places, people, and smells. A sheltered dog is a scared dog, and a scared dog is an aggressive one.

When a new person enters your home, never shut your Teacup Maltese into another room. This will only cause him to associate new people with isolation, and he will become even more aggressive. Instead, hold your dog on your lap. Talk to him, keeping your voice light and soothing. Allow him to sniff the other person. Keep the situation under control, and with time your Teacup Maltese will relax and learn to accept the presence of people as more or less normal.

As long as you desensitize your dog and reward him when he shows promising signs of improvement, within a matter of months, your dog will transform, and you'll be the proud owner of a happy, friendly Teacup Maltese.

# Chapter 12 – Maltese Dog Grooming: Pampered Or Practical?

***

One of my absolute favorite things about Teacup Maltese dogs is their long, pure white, silky coat. It's gorgeous and endearing; however, maintaining that coat takes a lot of time and effort.

## Coat Color—Black Maltese, White Maltese, Brown Maltese?

A quick word of caution, this is something you should keep in mind before you even bring home your Teacup Maltese. A purebred Maltese will always be white. There are no genetic color variations.

Some breeders might try to sell you a black Maltese, claiming that it is 'melanistic,' which is a genetic disorder similar to albinism where there are too many pigments in the hair or skin, resulting in a black dog. However, to my knowledge, there are no records of any melanistic Maltese dogs, Teacup or otherwise. More than likely this person is simply trying to sell you a black Maltese mix. Be careful when searching for a Teacup Maltese, and don't get swindled!

A breeder might do the same with a brown dog, claiming that it is a highly rare color variant of the Maltese. But don't be fooled.

A purebred Maltese will always be white, period.

## Maltese Grooming—The Basics

When it comes to your Teacup Maltese's coat, there're two options you can choose; long or short.

Naturally, Malteses have long, straight hair that looks and feels more like human hair than dog fur. Long hair is the typical 'look' of a Maltese; however, more and more people are opting to cut their Maltese's hair short, both for convenience and cleanliness.

*Long, straight, and silky smooth; the Teacup Maltese's coat, when*

*left in its natural state, is an incredibly beautiful sight!*

If you aren't going to have a lot of time or money to groom

your Teacup Maltese's coat often, you should consider opting for a puppy cut—a short cut that will keep all that extra hair from matting, tangling, or getting dirty. I personally prefer to keep all three of my dogs' hair long, but many people prefer the puppy cut.

Even if you clip his hair short, you will still have to brush your Teacup Maltese every day to ensure that his hair is clean, and his skin remains healthy.

If you decide to keep his hair long, then you have a lot of work ahead of you; however, the end result—a sleek, gorgeous dog—is well worth the extra effort. If you plan on entering your Teacup Maltese in dog shows, most likely this is the option you will have to go with.

Brush his coat every day. If you come across a mat or tangle, gently work through it with the comb and your fingers until it breaks apart. If necessary, spray it with a groomer-approved detangling spray. When you bathe him, use a doggy shampoo that deodorizes, cleans, and conditions to keep that coat smooth and silky.

Many people decide to keep their Maltese's long hair in a top knot. Not only does this keep the long hair out of the dog's eyes and away from his food when he eats, but it's also absolutely gorgeous and a key element to the Teacup Maltese's signature look. If you keep your Teacup Maltese's hair long, it's almost always expected to keep your dog's hair in a top knot.

To put your Teacup Maltese's hair in a top knot, first place your dog on an elevated surface, such as a tabletop, so that he's level with you. Using a comb, part the dog's hair in two places; starting at the bridge of his nose and ending with his head, creating the piece of hair you want to isolate. Gather the hair into one section and comb it so that it is sleek—if desired, backcomb the hair to create volume. Wrap a rubber band, one that won't pull your dog's hair, around the section, making sure that it isn't too tight and isn't pulling your dog's skin. Simply add a bow, if desired, and voila!

No matter what length you decide for your Teacup Maltese's coat, you will still have to bathe him often, at least once a week. Always make sure to protect his ear canals with cotton balls before you bathe him. Use lukewarm water; test the temperature like you would for an infant. If it seems hot to you, change the temperature. Teacup Malteses are sensitive little dogs, and you wouldn't want to burn their skin. Always use a dog-approved shampoo; don't break down and use your own, no matter how good it smells! This can dry out their skin and cause irritation.

You should take your Teacup Maltese to the groomer's at least once a month for a trim. You can do touch-ups in between his appointments, but it's a good idea to leave the heavy stuff up to the professionals.

*His coat may take a lot of work to upkeep,*
*but the end result is worth it!*

Trim your dog's nails often; if you can hear them clicking
on the floor, they're too long. It's important to keep his nails
short to avoid painful splitting and tearing. When
trimming, be careful to avoid the 'quick'; that is, the tissue
in your dog's nails that is comprised of blood vessels and
nerve endings. If his nails are light-colored, the quick is
easy to see, but if his nails are black avoiding the quick is
more difficult, and if you cut it, it can be extremely painful
for your dog. If you don't feel comfortable trimming them,
you can take ask your groomer or your vet to do it for you.

Always make sure the hair inside your Teacup Maltese's
ears is trimmed, and clean his ears often with a cotton
swab—gently, don't probe the ear canal or you could
inadvertently cause injury. It's important to keep his ears
clean to avoid bad odor and possible ear infections.

Brush your Teacup Maltese's teeth at least two or three times a week, more if possible. Never use toothpaste formulated for people; the ingredients used in human toothpaste can be toxic to dogs to swallow. Instead, buy a gentle doggy toothpaste from your local pet store. Likewise, use a toothbrush especially meant for dogs. Your dog might hate it at first, but if tooth brushing is a regular part of his routine, he'll soon become used to it.

All white dogs are prone to tear stains around their eyes. Gently clean the area around his eyes every day with cotton balls dipped in warm water to prevent them. Tear stains in and of themselves aren't harmful to your dog, but they are unsightly, and by cleaning your dog's eyes you can preserve the Miniature Maltese's unique stunning beauty.

All in all, these pampered little pups do require a bit more effort than your standard brown, flat-coated dog, but if you develop a schedule and a routine to maintain his health and appearance, you won't be overwhelmed with the demands of caring for such a beautiful dog.

## Chapter 13- Micro Maltese Life Expectancy and Old Age

***

Dogs are such a huge part of our lives. We love them and care for them as if they were a member of our families—and for many people, myself included, they are. We can do our best to make sure our dogs are as happy and healthy as possible, but it's a tragic and yet an unavoidable fact of life that people simply live longer than dogs.

Every pet owner dreads each passing year, for eventually, the day will come when we will have to say goodbye to our dogs. In fact, short lifespan is one of the reasons that some people choose not to own a dog; why welcome something into your life and love it if it's going to die much sooner than yourself?

The pain of losing a dog is enormous, but I couldn't imagine my life without them. They bring me so much joy. I'd rather live knowing that one day I will have to say goodbye to them than never have them at all. The pain is worth it, and that's true of love in general. Love doesn't come with a risk-free guarantee.

However, there's good news: With proper vet care and the right preventative measures taken early on in your dog's life, your Teacup Maltese can be expected to live for twelve years, possibly even longer—it's not unusual for a Teacup Maltese to live to be seventeen or eighteen.

Twelve years is short compared to our lifespans, but it's still an incredible amount of time to have your dog by your side.

One of the reasons I prefer a toy or small dogs is because most breeds follow a general rule of thumb; the smaller the dog, the longer it will live. Small breeds have a much longer expected lifespan than larger breeds. For instance, most small breeds have an average life expectancy of twelve to fourteen years; the Great Dane, one of the biggest breeds in the world, has a life expectancy of only seven years.

When you first bring a Teacup Maltese into your home, it's important to understand not only how long he will live, but how he will develop, both physically and mentally, with the passing of time.

It's a commonly held belief that every year equals seven 'dog years', and that when your puppy reaches his first year, he is seven in 'dog years,' then fourteen the next, and so on. Nearly everyone believes and recites this theory, but it simply isn't true. Dogs develop at different speeds than we do. When your Teacup Maltese turns a year old, he's already fully grown. How many people are fully grown at the age of seven?

*Of course, all dogs are really full-grown toddlers.
Everyone knows that!*

If you want to compare your dog's growth with that of a
human, remember that his life can't be broken down into an
even amount of 'dog years' with each passing year. Instead,
once he reaches his peak, at about a year or two, his
development slows down, and he ages at a slower pace.

To track your Teacup Maltese's growth and 'age', take a look at this table. (Note: This applies only to Teacup Maltese dogs. Other breeds may age differently.)

| Time | Teacup Maltese Age |
|---|---|
| 1 Year | 15 |
| 2 Years | 21 |
| 3 Years | 25 |
| 4 Years | 29 |
| 5 Years | 33 |
| 6 Years | 37 |
| 7 Years | 41 |
| 8 Years | 45 |
| 9 Years | 49 |
| 10 Years | 53 |
| 11 Years | 57 |
| 12 Years | 61 |
| 13 Years | 65 |
| 14 Years | 69 |
| 15 Years | 73 |
| 16 Years | 77 |
| 17 Years | 81 |
| 18 Years | 85 |
| 19 Years | 89 |
| 20 Years | 93 |

Obviously, these are arbitrary numbers, but you get a general idea. Dogs age extremely quickly in their first year or two; then after they hit their growth spurt they slow down and age at a slower pace.

One of the leading causes of death in older dogs is disease. Once your Teacup Maltese gets older his immune system weakens. This makes him more vulnerable not only to bacterial and viral infections but to diseases like cancer and heart disease.

However, fear not—there are steps you can take to protect your Teacup Maltese's health, whether he's a young, spry dog or an older, mature dog.

The most important thing you should do to save your pup from potentially fatal health problems is to take him to the vet twice a year for checkups, whether or not you think they are necessary. Many diseases are invisible until it's too late; your vet can perform blood tests and x-rays to make sure no nasty surprises are lingering in your Teacup Maltese's body. Also, make sure that your pup is always up to date on his vaccinations. Some of the deadliest canine diseases are easily preventable with regular shots.

One of the most common causes of death in older dogs, just like people, is cancer. If your dog has cancer, there might be measures your vet can take to save his life, depending on what sort of cancer he has and what stage it is in. However, this isn't always possible, so make sure you take as many steps as possible in preventing your dog from developing cancer in the first place.

- Spay or neuter your Teacup Maltese. Spaying and neutering can drastically reduce your pet's chances of developing certain types of cancer; spaying female dogs reduces the chance of mammary cancer and eliminates the possibility of ovarian and uterine cancer, and neutering male dogs reduces the chance of prostate cancer and other prostate diseases and eliminates the possibility of developing testicular cancer. (Also, unless you plan on breeding your Teacup Maltese, spaying and neutering is the right thing to do anyway).

- Don't smoke around your pet. If your Teacup Maltese is exposed to secondhand smoke, he runs the risk of developing lung cancer and heart disease. If you smoke, please do so outside if at all possible.

- Control your Teacup Maltese's diet and make sure he gets adequate exercise. This is a highly important step to preventing doggy cancer. Don't feed your dog people food, which may contain additives and cancer-causing carcinogens. Only feed him fresh food or food designed for dogs. Teacup Malteses aren't the most active of the toy breeds, but make sure he has at least some exercise every day, especially older dogs.

Dental care is crucial. Make sure you brush your Teacup Maltese's teeth often and take him to the vet for teeth cleanings. Unfortunately, many people seem to think that a dog's oral hygiene can be neglected; but if left unchecked, your dog can develop dental problems that can progress to infections, and these can be extremely deadly, especially for older dogs with weakened immune systems.

Some diseases are unavoidable, but by providing consistent vet care and taking precautions against cancer, you can help prolong your Teacup Maltese's life span.

If you have an elderly Teacup Maltese, it may be heartbreaking to see your once perky little dog become less playful and prone to long naps. There are several challenges associated with owning an older dog, but by changing up your lifestyle just a little bit, and by keeping a few things in mind, you can ensure that your Teacup Maltese will be as comfortable in his old age as possible.

If your Teacup Maltese is ten years old or older, he's considered a 'senior.'

When a dog gets older, his joints become weaker, and he may even develop arthritis. Keep him off of furniture and make sure he has a nice, soft bed; there are even dog beds available that are specially made for senior dogs.

You might want to consider feeding your elderly Teacup Maltese a specially formulated dog food that contains vitamins and minerals that are important to maintain a senior dog's health. When dogs age, their teeth tend to wear down, so make sure that his food is bite-sized, and he has no problems chewing when he eats.

Adjust his exercise needs. Exercise is still important to an elderly Teacup Maltese, but he shouldn't run and play as much, nor will he want to.

Unfortunately, blindness and deafness are common in older dogs. Adjust your lifestyle to his disabilities. Dogs seem to adjust to blindness and deafness better than people do, but it still might make life challenging for them. Ease their struggle by never startling a deaf dog, and remove obstacles around your home that might harm a blind dog.

It's important for you and your family to understand that your elderly Teacup Maltese simply isn't the dog he once was. He might become slightly irritable, which is understandable; be sure to give him his space. Likewise, he will spend a lot of time sleeping, and he will be a lot more sensitive to noise and change. Make sure to speak quietly around him and try your best not to startle him.

By understanding your Teacup Maltese's transition into old age, you can make sure that his final years are filled with love and comfort.

## Chapter 14 – To Show Or Not To Show?
## Dog Shows And Their Merits

***

A s a child, I was absolutely fascinated with dog shows. I would watch them whenever they came on television, enamored by the beauty and grace of all the breeds shown together in one ring. Right then and there, at the age of ten, I decided that I wanted a show dog when I became an adult.

Well, I definitely had no idea of just how much time, money, and effort it takes to obtain and maintain a high-quality show dog. It's a sport, plain and simple, and like any sport, you and your dog must work extremely hard in order to be considered to compete.

Unfortunately, most dog shows are conformation shows; meaning that the sole purpose of these shows is to display dogs that conform almost perfectly to breed standards. For that reason, you might not be able to enter your Teacup Maltese into a dog show.

The breed standard of a Maltese is 'less than seven pounds, with four to six being preferred'. If your Teacup Maltese weighs four pounds, he technically is within the boundaries, meaning that he can't be barred from being entered in a dog show based on his weight alone; although he'll still be considered a small Maltese, of course! However, four pounds is the absolute minimum, and if he weighs less than that he probably can't be entered in a dog show.

There're many, many more factors to consider before you can enter him in a show. Is he registered with the AKC (or the main kennel club of your country)? Is he from an excellent bloodline? Do you have the time and money to dedicate to grooming, show training, equipment, travel, and entry fees?

Show quality dogs, especially for such a high-end dog as the Maltese, cost a LOT. You might have to wait a long time before such a puppy becomes available through a breeder. However, if you don't want to buy a show dog, and you want to enter your own into a show, even if he's not from a champion bloodline, you can still enter him in smaller, local shows.

If you want to show your Teacup Maltese, don't get him/her spayed or neutered. Dog shows were originally created to showcase prime breeding stock, and that rule remains today; all dogs shown must be intact. If you choose not to spay or neuter your Teacup Maltese, make sure you remain responsible for your dog's reproductive health. If you have a female dog, don't allow her outside while she's in heat, and always make sure that you know where your dog is at all times. Please don't contribute to canine overpopulation.

Dog shows are a full-time sport. When you're not showing your dog, he has to stay in peak physical condition, and you can never relax his training routine.

If you plan on showing your Teacup Maltese, keep his hair long; don't trim it into a puppy cut. Brush it every single day and be sure to keep his eyes clean to avoid tear stains. Your groomer may recommend using a dog-friendly whitening shampoo that will keep his coat bright and spotless. Before shows, your groomer will most likely put your Teacup Maltese's hair into a top knot, so it's a good idea to get him used to one before he gets into a ring for the first time.

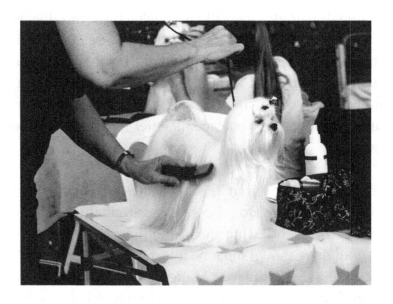

*Teacup Malteses: The stars of the show!*

There're so many things that you need to know before you decide to show your dog, but these are only the basics. The real point of this chapter highlights the pros and cons of dog shows.

The best thing about entering into a dog show, especially if your dog actually wins a ribbon, is the sheer honor. Not many people have bragging rights for a show dog. If your dog holds a title, he immediately becomes valuable in the eyes of breeders, meaning you can potentially earn some money if you decide to breed him and sell his puppies. He'll have a name for himself in the dog world, and dog shows teach him poise, grace, and discipline.

But dog shows are outrageously expensive, and you might go through all that effort with absolutely nothing to show for it.

When you get right down to it, a ribbon is just a ribbon. Your dog doesn't care either way; all he wants is love, and unfortunately for many people, the honor and prestige of owning a show dog overcomes their love for their pet. Your Teacup Maltese needs to know that he's loved and cherished, no matter what a piece of paper says.

Dog shows are a fun, exciting hobby, and you can learn so many things about other breeds by participating and watching dog shows. Dog shows are a tradition going back over a hundred years, and without them and the kennel clubs that sponsor them, many dog breeds simply wouldn't be the same today. But remember, to your dog, all the titles in the world couldn't make up for a family who loves him.

## Chapter 15 – Prospective Maltese Dog Breeders—What to Expect Breeding Teacup Maltese Dogs

***

**M**any people decide to breed their dogs as a form of passive income, but for me, it's not about the money; it's bringing joy to others in the form of a tiny, adorable Maltese puppy.

You might decide that your Teacup Maltese is ready to be bred; but before you do, remember that this isn't a decision to take lightly. There are millions of shelter dogs waiting for their forever home. Canine homelessness is such an epidemic that you shouldn't bring more puppies into this world unless you're absolutely sure that each and every one of them is going to a loving, responsible home.

You will be responsible for making sure that the puppies are healthy, that they get all of their shots, and that they are registered with the kennel club of your choice, if desired — not to mention ensure that both the puppies and the mother are comfortable during the eight or so weeks before the puppies will be old enough to be sold.

*Teacup Maltese puppies are some of the smallest in the world!*

If you have a male Teacup Maltese, the breeding process is relatively straightforward; once you work out an arrangement with the female Teacup Maltese's owner, they will most likely bring the female dog to your home when she goes into heat, and the breeding will take place there (some people prefer the opposite, with the male going to the female's house). Make sure that the breeding goes smoothly and that no other male dogs mate with the female. Then, when the puppies are born, you will either get the first pick of the litter or a portion of the money from puppy sales.

If you have a female Teacup Maltese, the process is much less straight-forward, and preparations must be made in advance.

First, make sure she's at a proper age. It's unhealthy for the mother and pups both for the mother to be bred before she's had her first complete heat cycle, although after her second is preferred; therefore, she should be bred when she's no younger than a year and a half old. Breeding her during her first heat cycle can cause serious complications during birth and the puppies' development. Also, I've found that generally mother dogs do better when they're bred later for the mere fact that they're more mature, and their motherly instincts are fully developed.

Now schedule an appointment with your vet. He will look over your dog to make sure that she's healthy, and perform tests to ensure she's free of any hereditary diseases that she might pass on to her pups. He will also assess her overall condition to make sure she can handle the strain of giving birth and nursing puppies. If he gives you the green light, you can progress to the next step.

Before your Teacup Maltese goes into heat, you should go ahead and find a 'stud,' which is the technical term for a male breeding dog. The technical term for a female breeding dog is 'bitch,' but I like to avoid that word as it definitely has negative connotations.

You can find many people advertising their studs online, or you can check with breeders in your area. Make sure that you get some sort of paperwork from the owner proving their dog's lineage and health. You might also want to meet the owner and the male Teacup Maltese beforehand to evaluate his temperament and personality.

It's definitely advisable to find a stud in your area, but that's not always possible. If he lives a long way from your home, you'll have to pay to fly your dog to him, which can get extremely expensive.

**Heat Cycles**

Your Teacup Maltese will first come into heat when she's about six months old. As stated earlier, DO NOT BREED HER ON HER FIRST HEAT. Most people agree that she shouldn't be bred on her second either; third heat, or when she's about one and a half to two years old, is best. During her first heat, and her second if you want her pregnancy to go as smoothly as possible, contain her in the house at all times; if she's outside, make sure she's on a leash, and she doesn't escape. Be careful during this time. Her scent will attract male dogs from miles around, and some of them might be territorial and aggressive.

While heat cycles vary from dog to dog, usually they last about 18 days and occur every six months, give or take.

Your Teacup Maltese will act differently while she's in heat; some get more aggressive, others more submissive. Most likely she will be restless; do your best to keep her comfortable during this time of change.

After about the 12th day, she's at her most fertile and should be bred. It's a good idea to take her to the vet first; he can perform tests on her to see when will be the best time to introduce her to the stud.

## Pregnancy

A few weeks after the mating has taken place, take your Teacup Maltese to the vet; he'll be able to perform either an ultrasound or a blood test to determine whether or not she's pregnant. If she is, congratulations! You can expect a litter of tiny, gorgeous Teacup Maltese puppies at about nine weeks after breeding, or 61-65 days.

Nine weeks is a short amount of time, and you'll need all that time to prepare yourself, your family, and the expectant mother for the new puppies.

First, increase the amount of food you give your Teacup Maltese; in fact, let her eat as much as she wants. She knows her body and knows how much she'll need to support her growing puppies.

Make sure she gets plenty of rest and doesn't overexert herself; however, gentle exercise is encouraged. Limit her activity to short walks, especially once she gets closer to the due date.

Discourage your Teacup Maltese from jumping off of furniture; this is recommended anyway, since they're tiny and could get injured, but it's even more important during her pregnancy.

Keep an eye out for warning signs of complications in her pregnancy, such as vaginal bleeding before she's due to give birth. If this happens, take her to the vet right away.

## Giving Birth

Once your Teacup Maltese reaches the 9-week mark, she's probably been miserable for weeks and ready for this pregnancy to be over! It's important to be patient with her and to help her along this uncomfortable process.

During the pregnancy, take her to the vet often for checkups and progress reports. He'll keep a good eye on her development and get an idea of when she's expected to give birth.

There's one thing you need to be prepared for. It's not uncommon, especially amongst small breeds like the Teacup Maltese, for the vet to recommend a Cesarean section. Many small dogs have severe difficulties while giving birth, and other factors might come into play that might require a Cesarean instead of a natural birth. Listen to your vet and trust his word. If he gives your Teacup Maltese the green light for a natural birth, you still need to be there for your dog in case of any complications.

A day before your dog goes into labor, she'll grow extremely restless. She might pace around the room, whine, refuse food, and begin looking for a place to 'nest'. Keep an eye out for these signs and be prepared. Prepare a whelping box—a cardboard or wooden box lined with blankets or towels placed in an area away from the main hustle and bustle of the house, preferably in a place where she's comfortable.

A day or so later, she will go into labor. Stay by her side the entire time. Just like humans, labor is painful for dogs. Some handle it better than others, but it's not unusual for dogs to whine or cry during birth. Encourage her and support her with pats and rubs. Unfortunately, there aren't any painkillers that are safe to give to dogs during this time. The best thing you can do for your dog is to be there for her.

Just like in humans, her water will break, and then the puppies will come one at a time. They will be encased in a birth sac, which the mother dog will normally break on her own; if she doesn't, it'll be up to you to gently extract the puppies from their sac and rub them dry with a towel. She will normally rest for about ten minutes between puppies until they're all born. If she doesn't sever the umbilical cord, snip it yourself with a pair of sanitized steel scissors. The placenta will be pushed out next. It's normal for dogs to eat the placenta, but if she doesn't, throw it away.

Check the puppies for any abnormalities. If they don't nurse, call your vet; he'll tell you what to do.

A normal Teacup Maltese litter should contain 3 or 4 puppies, although only one or two aren't unusual.

Take the new mother and her puppies to the vet after a few days to make sure that she's recovering well and that the puppies are healthy.

## Chapter 16 – Conclusion

\*\*\*

ll in all, a Teacup Maltese is, in my opinion, the best dog on the planet. Beauty, dignity, poise, love, and undying loyalty to the people willing to let them into their hearts are wrapped up in one tiny, dainty little package. Who could ask for a better dog?

With that being said, they do require a little more attention and effort than other breeds. It's a sad, sad occasion when I see a Maltese at my local animal shelter, abandoned because its owner simply didn't understand these dogs, where they came from, and what they need in this world. Dogs are living, breathing animals, not decorations, and unfortunately, many people see them as just that. They're beautiful creatures, and they deserve every single ounce of love and care that we can give them.

*Bright eyes, a wagging tail, and lifelong love and loyalty;
what more could you ask for in a dog?*

I wrote this book to share with the world my love and admiration for this dog and to educate anyone who is interested in bringing one into their lives. It was a journey that I'm blessed to have been a part of, for I learned much from myself and my own dogs.

Please be responsible about breeding or buying Teacup Malteses, and always remember that your little bundle of fur only wants your love.

I'm honored to have been given the opportunity to research

and write about the breed I love so much, and if this book has convinced you to open your heart and your home to a Teacup Maltese, I can consider my job done.

# A

# B

# C

# D

# E

exercise · 57, 70, 90, 107, 108, 118
exotic · 16

# F

fatal · 64, 77, 81, 85, 106
feeding · 11, 62, 67, 68, 70, 71, 74, 108
fence · 58, 80
fertile · 117
fleas · 48, 84
Fleas · 84
food · 44, 62, 63, 68, 69, 70, 71, 72, 73, 74, 76, 89, 98, 107, 108, 118, 119
full-grown · 36, 37, 104
fur · 21, 53, 57, 97, 122

# G

genes · 18, 50, 53
genetic disorders · 42
gingivitis · 84
Glaucoma · 82
grooming · 11, 33, 34, 45, 64, 111

# H

*hair* · 17, 34, 53, 58, 71, 84, 86, 96, 97, 98, 100, 112
harness · 66
health · 22, 23, 39, 42, 59, 64, 70, 78, 79, 85, 101, 106, 108, 111, 116
Heart disease · 81
heat cycle · 45, 116
Hepatitis · 85
hereditary diseases · 116
history · 14, 15, 16, 18, 39, 81
homemade food · 73
housetraining · 88, 89
hybrid dogs · *See* designer breeds
hyperactive · 27, 69
hypoallergenic · 34, 50, 52
hypoglycemia · 71, 73

# I

ID tag · 65
inbred · 21
independent · 55, 56
injury · 79, 80, 81, 100
intelligent · 52, 55, 57, 58
internal infection · 23
Italy · 14, 15

# K

kennel clubs · 18, 51, 113
kilograms · 19, 23, 54, 58

# L

labor · 119, 120
Labradoodle · 50, 51
lethargic · 22
life expectancy · 103
lineage · 116
litter · 26, 115, 118, 120
love · 9, 11, 12, 13, 23, 28, 29, 31, 32, 37, 48, 52, 55, 58, 90, 102, 109, 113, 121, 122, 123

# M

Malchi · 54, 55
Malta · 15
Malteagle · 56, 57
Maltese · 11, 13, 14, 15, 16, 17, 18, 19, 20, 23, 25, 27, 30, 32, 34, 36, 38, 39, 43, 51, 52, 53, 54, 55, 56, 57, 58, 61, 63, 64, 65, 66, 69, 75, 78, 79, 80, 81, 86, 88, 93, 94, 95, 96, 97, 98, 102, 103, 105, 107, 108, 110, 111, 112, 114, 115, 118, 119, 121
Maltese dogs · 9, 12, 13, 14, 15, 17, 18, 21, 24, 26, 37, 38, 79, 80, 81, 83, 86, 92, 96, 105
Maltese Lion Dog · 16
Maltichon · 53
Maltipom · 56
Maltipoo · 11, 33, 52, 53
mange · 84

# R

# S

stud · 117
surgery · 82

# T

# U

United States · 25, 30, 43
urine · 44, 47, 90
USA · *See* United States

# V

vaccines · 85
variation · 14, 18, 38
vet · 22, 23, 36, 40, 45, 48, 49, 62, 65, 73, 78, 79, 81, 82, 83, 84, 85, 89, 100, 103,
    106, 107, 108, 116, 117, 118, 119, 120
veterinarian · 47, 72, 79, 84
vision loss · 83

# W

walk · 27, 66
weight · 70, 73, 111
whelping box · 119
white · 15, 28, 34, 48, 53, 54, 74, 96, 97, 101
White Shaker Dog Syndrome · 83

# X

x-rays · 106

Dr. Marly

# Pet Food not Good
# Ingredients

BHA, Fillers, Grains Good
Brown Rice

'Bad'
Corn-Bad
Gluten
Soy Bean oil

Barly Oatmed
white rice

Bad grams
Heavy
Grains
wheat
Flour

Have Veggies is good

have
Presative free
(Meat By Products) colors
Bad For dog

Ducks, Chicken    this meat
By product      Never feed
Meal Meal        your dog
or
Bone meal
Bad    Best meat

ox meaty

# Pet Food not Good
## ingredients

wheat

How much
Protien in dogs diet

By Product, Preservatives, Fillers
Are Bad

- 3 Super nutrients - Good for dogs
organ meat - Great Vitamins, Nutrients
omgea threes, Fatty acid -

PrEBiotics - Super food For Gut Bacteria
Flax, Pea Flour,
Seratonin - made in Digestion Better

taurine is good for dogs
is a Vitamin
---

High Quality
turkey heart, Beef liver EPA, DHA
Veggles, Fruits
Polyphenols
Ginger - Joint Health, turkey heart
tocorahals

Dr. marty NaturesBlend
Freeze dried Dog Food

# Dr. martys Natures Blend
## Freeze Dried dog Food as Food topper
us a
over a dog food
You Bought

16 oz  29.95
Bag

order
in 3 pack - 6 pack

subscription order

Raw turkey
Duck
Salmon
Sweet Potatos
BlueBerries/cranberries
spinach
Ginger, Flax
ETC!

My Dog treats # Customer Care team
800 829 4493

74106210R00075

Dogs Food Kind

Wieght adult About 6 lbs Dry food 248 cal
Can food 232
other fresh 220
Food